Transforming Primary QTS

Teaching Arithmetic in Primary Schools

Transforming Primary QTS

Teaching Arithmetic in Primary Schools

Richard English

Series Editor: Alice Hansen

Los Angeles | London | New Delhi
Singapore | Washington DC

Learning Matters
An imprint of SAGE Publications Ltd
1 Oliver's Yard
55 City Road
London EC1Y 1SP

SAGE Publications Inc.
2455 Teller Road
Thousand Oaks, California 91320

SAGE Publications India Pvt Ltd
B 1/I 1 Mohan Cooperative Industrial Area
Mathura Road
New Delhi 110 044

SAGE Asia-Pacific Pte Ltd
3 Church Street
#10-04 Samsung Hub
Singapore 049483

Editor: Amy Thornton
Development Editor: Jennifer Clark
Production Controller: Chris Marke
Project Management: Deer Park Productions
Marketing Manager: Catherine Slinn
Cover design: Wendy Scott
Typeset by: PDQ Typesetting Ltd
Printed and bound in Great Britain by: MPG Books
Group, Bodmin, Cornwall

© 2013 Richard English

First published in 2013

Apart from any fair dealing for the purposes of research
or private study, or criticism or review, as permitted
under the Copyright, Designs and Patents Act, 1988,
this publication may be reproduced, stored or
transmitted in any form, or by any means, only with
the prior permission in writing of the publishers, or in
the case of reprographic reproduction, in accordance
with the terms of licences issued by the Copyright
Licensing Agency. Enquiries concerning reproduction
outside those terms should be sent to the publishers.

Library of Congress Control Number: 2012945181

British Library Cataloguing in Publication data

A catalogue record for this book is available from the
British Library

ISBN 978 0 85725 725 3 paperback
ISBN 978 0 85725 855 7 hardback

MIX
Paper from
responsible sources
FSC® C018575

BATH SPA UNIVERSITY
NEWTON PARK LIBRARY
Class No.
372 ENG
DISCARD
20/12/12

Contents

About the author   vi

Introduction   1

1.   Getting your head around arithmetic   3

2.   The rapid recall of number facts   15

3.   Mental arithmetic   24

4.   The development of pencil and paper arithmetic   41

5.   Traditional pencil and paper arithmetic   64

6.   Arithmetic with fractions, decimals, percentages
     and ratios   89

7.   Arithmetic using technology   116

     *Appendix: Model answers to the self-assessment
     questions*   139

     Index   149

The author

For the past 18 years Richard English has been a primary mathematics tutor in the Faculty of Education at the University of Hull. Prior to that he taught mathematics in primary and secondary schools in Hull and had also worked as a mathematics advisory teacher. In recent years he has worked on a consultancy basis for the National Strategies and was involved in the early development of the mathematics specialist training programme, following the publication of the Williams Review in 2008.

Series editor

Alice Hansen is the Director of Children Count Ltd where she is an educational consultant. Her work includes running professional development courses and events for teachers and teacher trainers, research and publishing. Alice has worked in education in England and abroad. Prior to her current work she was a primary mathematics tutor and the programme leader for a full-time primary PGCE programme at the University of Cumbria.

Introduction

This book is one of the first in the new *Transforming Primary QTS* series, which has been established to reflect current best practice and a more creative and integrated approach to the primary school curriculum.

It is vitally important that children develop arithmetical competence during their time in primary school. It provides them with the means to explore other aspects of mathematics and facilitates learning right across the curriculum. It also provides the foundations for the mathematics they will encounter in secondary school and equips them for their everyday lives, both as children and adults. With so much at stake in terms of children's development, this places a great deal of responsibility on schools to ensure that arithmetic teaching is of the highest quality. The overall aim of this book is therefore to equip you, as a trainee teacher, to teach arithmetic more effectively in the primary school.

About the book

The view of arithmetic presented in this book is not one based solely on the memorising of rules and procedures. Instead, there is a strong emphasis on arithmetical understanding, so that a range of mental, written and technology-based techniques can be applied flexibly to tackle any calculation. The development of your own subject knowledge is a key feature of the book and so you will find out how to perform many different arithmetical procedures, but always with an appreciation of how and why these work as well as the mathematical principles that underpin them. However, subject knowledge on its own is not sufficient and so pedagogical considerations feature strongly as well, but always based on the research, evaluation and inspection evidence that is available in the field of mathematics, together with numerous case studies of events that have taken place in primary classrooms. Finally, it would be inappropriate to consider the teaching of arithmetic without acknowledging the statutory obligations that schools and teachers must address and so the current and likely future curriculum expectations are discussed.

Using this book

Each chapter starts by identifying the learning outcomes and concludes by reviewing these and presenting self-assessment questions for you to tackle. The solutions to these questions are provided separately in the Appendix. The main body of each chapter focuses on the subject knowledge and pedagogical considerations associated with that particular aspect of arithmetic. There are activities for you to try along the way, which may require you to carry out an arithmetical task, or to reflect on your own capabilities or your experiences in school. Case studies feature in Chapters 2 to 7, so that you can see how the subject and pedagogical underpinnings translate into actual classroom practice. The case studies are often used to highlight common errors and misconceptions and so provide an opportunity for you to reflect on how you would deal with these. As a busy trainee teacher, caught up in the hurly-burly of the classroom, it is tempting to focus only on what is happening in your own school and so not reflect on the bigger picture beyond. This is why each chapter has a research focus, firstly so that you can see how the content presented in the chapter is underpinned by research, but secondly, and perhaps more importantly, so that you continue to engage with research throughout your teaching career and use it to inform your practice.

I hope you enjoy reading this book (I have certainly enjoyed writing it!) and I would like to think that it contributes to the development of your own subject and pedagogical knowledge, thus making you a more effective teacher.

1. Getting your head around arithmetic

Learning Outcomes

By the end of this chapter you will:

- have a clearer understanding of what is meant by the terms 'arithmetic', 'numeracy' and 'mathematics', both in a historical context and in relation to this book;
- be aware of the past, current and likely future curricular requirements in relation to arithmetic;
- understand the key issues and challenges facing primary schools in relation to the teaching of arithmetic.

What is arithmetic?

A good starting point for a book about arithmetic is a consideration of what we understand it to mean. Before discussing the historical interpretations and the interpretation used throughout the rest of this book, let us first see what your thoughts are about arithmetic.

Activity

What is your definition of arithmetic? Think about it for a few minutes and jot down a few notes. What experiences and recollections, possibly from your childhood, have informed your view of what constitutes arithmetic?

There is a strong possibility that your definition relates to calculation, perhaps with a particular emphasis on mental arithmetic and traditional pencil and paper procedures with the numbers set out one underneath the other. You may even recall having a weekly mental arithmetic test when you were a child at school, although I wonder if you were actually taught how to calculate mentally. In my own experience children were expected to perform well in mental arithmetic tests, but were never taught the necessary skills and techniques. A parallel situation would be to expect someone to do a driving test without having had any driving lessons!

Arithmetic, mathematics and numeracy

Arithmetic is a word usually associated with bygone days and this would seem to be supported by quotations provided in the introductory section of the Cockcroft Report (DES, 1982, page xii). One of these originates from Her Majesty's Inspectors in 1876, who state that *In arithmetic, I regret to say, worse results than ever before have been obtained.* Another is an extract from a Board of Education Report of 1925, which states that *Many have experienced some uneasiness about the condition of arithmetical knowledge and teaching at the present time.* A third quotation is from a Mathematical Association report of 1954:

> *Experience shows that a large proportion of entrants* [to trade courses] *have forgotten how to deal with simple vulgar and decimal fractions, have very hazy ideas on some easy arithmetical processes, and retain no knowledge of algebra, graphs or geometry, if, in fact, they ever did possess any.*

(DES, 1982, page xii)

If you would like to read more examples of the historical debate about mathematical education in the primary school, dip into a very interesting article by Alistair McIntosh (1981), details of which can be found in the Further Reading section at the end of this chapter.

The quotations presented above, perhaps in conjunction with your own reflections, lead to the conclusion that arithmetic relates to the mechanical processes of adding, subtracting, multiplying and dividing, either mentally or using pencil and paper. Importantly, this view of arithmetic is usually associated with a complete absence of any understanding of the underlying processes involved in its execution. Arithmetic was seen as a set of rules and procedures, which, if followed precisely, would yield correct answers, but often at the expense of much anxiety on the part of those executing them. Arithmetic in this sense is therefore a subset of mathematics, and indeed is not even a complete representation of what we usually refer to as number work.

The shift away from the widespread use of the word 'arithmetic' came about in the 1960s and 1970s with the advent of initiatives such as the Nuffield Mathematics Teaching Project from 1964 to 1971 and the publication of the Plowden Report in 1967. The widening of the mathematics curriculum and the move towards pupil-centred, as opposed to teacher-centred, education resulted in the expression 'arithmetic' no longer being an accurate representation of children's experiences, and as a consequence it fell out of favour.

The expression 'numeracy' became popular in the 1990s with the introduction of the National Numeracy Project in September 1996. This pilot project, the forerunner of the National Numeracy Strategy, had a clear focus on the development of number skills and solving number problems, and so the first Numeracy Framework made no reference at all to areas of mathematics such as shape, space, measures or handling data. The definition of numeracy was modified further in The Final Report of the Numeracy Task Force, which presented it as being:

> *A proficiency that involves a confidence and competence with numbers and measures. It requires an understanding of the number system, a repertoire of computational skills and an inclination and ability to solve number problems in a variety of contexts. Numeracy also demands practical understanding of the ways in which information is gathered by counting and measuring, and is presented in graphs, diagrams, charts and tables.*

(DfEE, 1998, page 11)

This much broader definition of numeracy, together with the subsequent publication of the Framework for Teaching Mathematics (DfEE, 1999), indicates a complete blurring of the boundaries between what is understood by the terms numeracy and mathematics; they had, in effect, come to mean the same thing, certainly in the primary phase, if not more widely.

With regard to the falling out of favour of the expression 'arithmetic', it should be noted that this word appears not even once in either the 1999 version or the 2006 version of the Framework for Teaching Mathematics. However, since the change of government in May 2010 and the demise of the National Strategies in March 2011, the word has acquired new found popularity, even if only among politicians. Shortly before the 2010 election, the shadow schools secretary, Michael Gove, stated in an interview to *The Times* newspaper that:

> *Most parents would rather their children had a traditional education, with children sitting in rows, learning the kings and queens of England, the great works of literature, proper mental arithmetic, algebra by the age of 11, modern foreign languages. That's the best training for the mind and that's how children will be able to compete.*

> (Thomson and Sylvester, 2010)

and more recently, government schools minister, Nick Gibb, has stated that:

> *Our reforms will give all pupils a solid grounding in reading and arithmetic, with the right catch-up support if they start to fall behind.*

> (Paton, 2011)

Current and future statutory requirements in relation to mathematics and arithmetic will be considered later in this chapter and indeed throughout this book, although for the time being I will leave you to ponder on what is meant by 'proper mental arithmetic'.

One final observation with regard to the resurgence in the use of the word 'arithmetic': the word is not used at all in Ofsted's 2008 and 2009 reports about mathematics, but occurs frequently in the 2011 report, although this is not surprising given that:

> *This survey was conducted following a ministerial request for Ofsted to provide evidence on effective practice in the teaching of early arithmetic.*

> (Ofsted, 2011, page 5)

This resurgence in the use of the word 'arithmetic' is the reason why it features in the title of this book, but in doing so, one of the aims is to encourage teachers to move away from the narrow interpretations typically associated with the word.

The scope of arithmetic as presented in this book

Unlike the definitions of arithmetic discussed above, this book will adopt a broader interpretation. Yes, it will focus on calculations involving the four arithmetical operations, but there will also be a strong emphasis on arithmetical understanding, as well as clear progression in the development of arithmetical techniques. This will begin with the recall of number facts in Chapter 2, followed by a detailed examination of mental arithmetic in Chapter 3, where a guiding principle will be that existing facts can be utilised flexibly in many different ways to mentally juggle with numbers. This flexible approach to arithmetic, which will depend on the numbers involved as well as personal choice, could not be further removed from the notion of blindly following memorised rules and procedures, as is the case with the traditional view of arithmetic. The same is true of the development of pencil and paper arithmetic presented in Chapters 4 and 5. Here, the rules that are the traditional algorithms, which depend on memory rather than understanding, are viewed as possible endpoints in children's arithmetical progression, not the starting points. The beginnings of pencil and paper arithmetic are therefore examined first in Chapter 4, building on the flexible mental methods presented earlier. Even when traditional pencil and paper arithmetic is introduced in Chapter 5 there continues to be an emphasis on understanding how these compact, efficient procedures actually work, so as to help you to move away from the notion of blindly following rules. Chapter 6 considers arithmetic involving fractions, decimals, percentages and ratios, and it makes use of the full range of arithmetical techniques discussed in Chapters 2 to 5. Finally, in Chapter 7, the vitally important role of technology is discussed, with a particular emphasis on calculators and spreadsheets.

Research Focus: Relational and instrumental understanding

Richard Skemp's seminal article, first published in 1977, presents two contrasting views of mathematical understanding: relational (*knowing both what to do and why*) and instrumental (*rules without reasons*), although it could be argued that the latter does not represent understanding at all. Examples of instrumental understanding include:

- the process of borrowing when using the traditional written method for subtraction;
- turning the fraction upside down and multiplying, when dividing by a fraction;
- taking a number across to the other side and changing the sign when solving equations;
- remembering that a minus and a minus is a plus when dealing with negative numbers.

$\rightarrow$

Skemp argues that teachers and children will differ in their goals with regard to mathematical understanding. This can cause particular difficulties if the teacher is striving for relational understanding but the child is aiming for instrumental understanding ('Just tell me the rule!'). Likewise, there will be a similar conflict if the mathematical understanding goals are reversed, that is, the teacher just wants to teach rules, but the child is striving for relational understanding.

Skemp also discusses the advantages and disadvantages of each type of understanding. For example, instrumental mathematics is easier to grasp, it can be taught quickly and the rewards can be reaped almost immediately. In other words, you can learn the method and get a page of correct answers in no time at all. It is for these reasons, combined with the pressure of exams and getting through the syllabus, that many teachers choose instrumental understanding as the goal for their children.

Regarding the limitations of instrumental understanding Skemp describes a scenario in which two people are visiting an unfamiliar town. One has separate detailed sets of instructions to get to and from various locations in the town. The other has explored the town, familiarised himself with the roads and built up a mental map of where everything is. The first person is all right as long as he follows the instructions precisely, but if at any time he takes a wrong turn he will be lost and will remain lost until he retraces his steps and starts again. In contrast, the second person's mental map provides him with an infinite number of possibilities which will allow him to get from any starting point to any finishing point and, as Skemp states:

> If he does take a wrong turn, he will still know where he is, and thereby be able to correct his mistake without getting lost; even perhaps to learn from it.

(1997, page 22)

If you are unable to obtain a copy of Skemp's article, instead read Chapter 1 of O'Sullivan et al. (2005), which presents and discusses a large extract from the original.

Curricular requirements for arithmetic

Before presenting the government's current priorities for arithmetic, it is worth examining the statutory requirements as they have developed over the last 25 years.

Recall of number facts

In terms of statutory National Curriculum requirements since 1989 there has been a consistent expectation with regard to children's recall of number facts. All versions of the programmes of study have indicated that children, by the time they leave primary school, should be able to recall addition and subtraction facts for numbers up to 20 and multiplication facts up to 10 × 10 (DES, 1989; DfEE/QCA, 1999).

Mental arithmetic

The first version of the National Curriculum (DES, 1989) required children to:

- add or subtract mentally two two-digit numbers;
- add mentally several single-digit numbers.

The new National Curriculum, implemented from September 2000 (DfEE/QCA, 1999), provided more detail with regard to mental arithmetic, with children being expected to:

- add or subtract any pair of two-digit whole numbers;
- cope with particular cases of three-digit and four-digit additions and subtractions (for example 3000 − 1997);
- double and halve any two-digit number;
- multiply and divide, initially in the range 1 to 100 (i.e. multiply or divide a two-digit number by a single digit number) and then for particular cases of larger numbers.

The National Curriculum programmes of study have always had to maintain a delicate balancing act, whereby sufficient detail is provided to ensure everyone is clear about the expectations, while at the same time producing a document which is concise and manageable for teachers. It is therefore impractical to provide more detail and exemplification than is summarised above, although the framework documents published by the National Numeracy Strategy and the Primary Strategies were able to accomplish this. Bearing this in mind, and also acknowledging that the programme of study represents only a minimum entitlement for children, the curriculum requirements listed above appear to be placing a sufficiently strong emphasis on mental arithmetic.

Pencil and paper arithmetic

The first National Curriculum (DES, 1989) required children to:

- use non-calculator methods to add and subtract two three-digit numbers;
- use non-calculator methods to multiply a three-digit number by a two-digit number and divide a three-digit number by a two-digit number.

As with mental arithmetic, the later version (DfEE/QCA, 1999) provided greater detail, with children being expected to:

- use written methods to add and subtract positive integers less than 1000, then up to 10,000;
- use written methods to add and subtract numbers involving decimals;

- use written methods for short multiplication and division to multiply and divide two-digit, three-digit and four-digit numbers by a single digit;
- use written methods for short multiplication and division to multiply and divide decimal numbers by a single digit;
- use written methods for long multiplication to multiply a three-digit number by a two-digit number;
- extend division to informal methods for dividing by a two-digit number.

It is interesting to note the subtle change of language from the first to the second version of the National Curriculum, with 'non-calculator' methods being replaced by 'written methods'. It could be argued that the first version seems to be promoting informal written approaches more than the second. Expressions such as 'written methods for long multiplication' conjure up images of the traditional approach, with the digits arranged in columns in anticipation of the 'carrying' that is likely to follow. However, another interpretation is that given there is no specific mention of 'traditional' or 'compact' written methods, this provides the opportunity for teachers to introduce informal methods which initially build on children's mental skills and bear no resemblance to the traditional approaches which will be encountered later.

The curriculum that never was

Prior to the change of government in May 2010, teachers were preparing for a new National Curriculum to be introduced in September 2011. The new programme of study for mathematics (QCDA, 2010) indicated that children should be taught to:

- know multiplication facts to 10×10;
- develop a range of strategies for calculating and checking (this includes mental methods, informal and formal written methods and using technology).

This represented a reduction in the level of detail presented in earlier versions, therefore providing greater scope when interpreting the requirements. The other notable feature is the more explicit acknowledgement of informal written methods.

Looking towards the future

Early in 2012 the government gave some indication of its current priorities for arithmetic, as follows.

- *Children must be able to recall quickly and accurately basic 'number facts' (e.g. number bonds and multiplication tables).*
- *Children must be fluent in applying quick, efficient written methods of calculation.*
- *Children need to be moved on rapidly to use appropriate efficient written methods, rather than becoming dependent on intermediate methods. This should be reflected*

in school policy. No child should be labouring with interim calculation methods in the long term.

- *Children need to understand and use the mathematical concepts that underpin number and arithmetic, such as place value and proportion. Without such concepts, pupils are ultimately less able to perform mental or written calculations, solve problems and reason mathematically.*

- *All children must leave primary school both proficient in the school's arithmetical algorithm for each operation and with a good understanding of the underpinning mathematics, both of which will equip them for solving unfamiliar problems and as a foundation for the more complex mathematics they will be taught in secondary school.*

(DfE, 2012a)

These priorities will be discussed in more detail at appropriate points throughout this book, although at this stage it is worth making the important point that there is no reference at all to mental calculation and only a passing acknowledgement of informal pencil and paper methods (referred to as 'intermediate' and 'interim' methods above).

In June 2012 the DfE published draft programmes of study for mathematics (DfE, 2012b) which provide more details of the proposed national curriculum which will be in place from September 2014. The draft programmes of study reflect the government priorities identified earlier, but additionally they do acknowledge the importance of mental arithmetic across the whole of the primary age range. However, there is minimal reference to informal pencil and paper methods. Instead the terms 'reliable' and 'efficient' written methods are used occasionally, but the expression 'formal written methods' is more predominant from Year 3 onwards. It is also noticeable that compared to the current and former versions of the national curriculum, traditional pencil and paper arithmetic in vertical columns is introduced at a much earlier age.

Both the March 2012 government priorities and the June 2012 draft programmes of study indicate that schools will be given a degree of flexibility when devising and implementing the mathematics curriculum, including their policies for arithmetic. In doing so, it is hoped that the wealth of research evidence clearly demonstrating the crucial role of approaches other than formal written methods, is acknowledged by schools. Thus a broader and more balanced interpretation of arithmetic, in tune with the one presented in this book, will inform classroom practice.

Children's attainment in arithmetic

Attempts to compare children's levels of attainment across different time periods are fraught with the same difficulties as when making comparisons of sporting excellence through the ages. Who is the greatest goal-scorer the footballing world has ever seen? On current form you might say Lionel Messi, although a few years ago perhaps Thierry Henry. Go further back in time and it might be Marco van Basten, or Diego Maradona, or George Best, or Pele, or Ferenc Puskás. The simple fact is that it is impossible to make meaningful comparisons, because these cannot possibly take account of the context in which each individual player was excelling. The same is true of pupil attainment. It is therefore a complete waste of time and effort to attempt to compare standards now with those in the 1990s or before. Even during a period when, supposedly, the same instruments have been used to measure attainment, the comparisons need to be viewed with caution. The proportion of children achieving the highest grades in GCSE mathematics has risen steadily over the years, but there are many who would argue that it is far easier to be awarded a grade C now than it was in the 1980s. Similarly with Key Stage 2 National Tests results, the percentage of children achieving level 4 or above has risen from 44 per cent in 1995 to 80 per cent in 2011, and yet there have been constant cries throughout this period proclaiming that standards need to be raised further, or that school leavers lack basic skills, or that pupils in other countries perform better than ours in international tests, or that the quality of teaching needs to be improved. There is certainly no room for complacency, but I would suggest that things are sometimes not as bad as the headlines would suggest, and it is a fact of life that people look back to bygone days through rose-tinted spectacles and so are perpetually critical of their current lot. Cockcroft (DES, 1982, page xiii) recognised this thirty years ago when he observed that *criticism of mathematics teaching is not new* and it is likely that he would reach the same conclusion today.

Current issues and challenges

Despite the cautionary words above, it is appropriate to identify the issues that need to be addressed if we want to improve the overall quality of children's arithmetical capability in the primary school. The following list focuses specifically on issues relating to arithmetic, rather than broader mathematical concerns, and is based on several recent publications from Ofsted, as well as other government sources.

- It is essential that children are able to recall number facts, such as multiplication tables and number bonds, because these, together with an understanding of place value, lay the foundations for mental and pencil and paper arithmetic (DfES, 2007; DCSF, 2007; Ofsted, 2011).

- Greater emphasis should be given to the development of children's mental arithmetic skills and this must be maintained throughout the primary years, even after written methods have been introduced (DfES, 2007; DCSF, 2007; DCSF, 2008).

- Children should not use written or calculator methods for calculations that can be done mentally (DfES, 2007; DCSF, 2007; Ofsted, 2008).

- Arithmetical understanding should be developed through high-quality questioning and discussion, rather than simply presenting rules and procedures to be memorised (DCSF, 2007; DCSF, 2008; Ofsted, 2008).

- Individual arithmetical methods and operations should not be considered in isolation. Instead, children need to be made aware of the connections and relationships that exist between the methods they are learning and between the four arithmetical operations (DCSF, 2007; DCSF, 2008; Ofsted, 2008; Ofsted, 2011).

- Greater use needs to be made of practical resources and visual aids to support the teaching of arithmetic (DfES, 2007; DCSF, 2007; DCSF, 2008; Ofsted, 2008; Ofsted, 2009; Ofsted, 2011).

- Children must be to taught how to use calculators more effectively (DCSF, 2007; Ofsted, 2011).

- More opportunities need to be provided to allow children to use and apply their arithmetical skills through problem solving and open-ended, investigative tasks, as well as through cross-curricular activities (DfES, 2007; DCSF, 2007; DCSF, 2008; Ofsted, 2008; Ofsted, 2009; Ofsted, 2011).

- Teachers need to have the necessary subject and pedagogical knowledge to address the issues listed above (DCSF, 2008; Ofsted, 2008; Ofsted, 2009; Ofsted, 2011).

The remaining chapters of this book aim to address the final bullet point above, so that you will be suitably equipped to meet the challenges you face in teaching arithmetic in the primary school.

Learning Outcomes Review

It is hoped that this introductory chapter has set the scene for you in terms of what is meant by arithmetic and the extent to which it features in the current and likely future curriculum requirements. The historical perspectives presented should also have contributed to your overall understanding of the issues surrounding the teaching of arithmetic. However, the most important aspect of this chapter is that it has identified for you the key challenges facing schools and teachers if they want to develop children's arithmetical capability. The remainder of this book will help you to meet these challenges.

Further Reading

Brown, M. (2010) Swings and roundabouts in Thompson, I. (ed.) *Issues in Teaching Numeracy in Primary Schools*. Maidenhead: Open University Press.

McIntosh, A. (1981) When will they ever learn? in Floyd, A. (ed.) *Developing Mathematical Thinking*. London: Addison-Wesley Publishers.

O'Sullivan, L., Harris, A., Sangster, M., Wild, J., Donaldson, G. and Bottle, G. (2005) *Primary Mathematics: Reflective Reader*. Exeter: Learning Matters. Read Chapter 1 ('The nature of mathematical understanding').

References

DCSF (2007) *Getting There – Able pupils who lose momentum in English and Mathematics in Key Stage 2*. Nottingham: DCSF Publications.

DCSF (2008) *Independent Review of Mathematics Teaching in Early Years Settings and Primary Schools* (The Williams Review). Nottingham: DCSF Publications.

DES (1982) *Mathematics Counts: Report of the Committee of Inquiry into the Teaching of Mathematics in Schools* (The Cockcroft Report). London: HMSO.

DES (1989) *Mathematics in the National Curriculum*. London: HMSO.

DfE (2012a) *Key priorities for arithmetic*. Presentation to ITT mathematics tutors, TDA/UCET/NASBTT conference for Primary ITT tutors, Lancaster and London. March, 2012.

DfE (2012b) *National Curriculum for Mathematics: Key Stages 1 and 2 – Draft*. London: DfE Publications.

DfEE (1998) *The Implementation of the National Numeracy Strategy: The Final Report of the Numeracy Task Force*. Sudbury: DfEE Publications.

DfEE (1999) *The National Numeracy Strategy: Framework for Teaching Mathematics*. Sudbury: DfEE Publications.

DfEE/QCA (1999) *The National Curriculum: Handbook for Primary Teachers in England*. London: HMSO.

DfES (2007) *Keeping Up – Pupils who fall behind in Key Stage 2*. Nottingham: DfES Publications.

Ofsted (2008) *Mathematics: Understanding the Score*. London: Ofsted Publications.

Ofsted (2009) *Understanding the Score: Improving practice in mathematics teaching at primary level*. London: Ofsted Publications.

Ofsted (2011) *Good Practice in Primary Mathematics: Evidence from 20 successful schools*. Manchester: Ofsted Publications.

O'Sullivan, L., Harris, A., Sangster, M., Wild, J., Donaldson, G. and Bottle, G. (2005) *Primary Mathematics: Reflective Reader*. Exeter: Learning Matters.

Paton, G. (2011) Thousands of children 'fail to make progress in three-Rs'. *Telegraph*, 9 June. Available at: www.telegraph.co.uk/education.educationnews/8565949/Thousands-of-children-fail-to-make-progress-in-the-three-Rs.html (accessed June 2012).

QCDA (2010) *The National Curriculum Primary Handbook*. Coventry: Qualifications and Curriculum Development Agency.

Skemp, R. (1977) Relational understanding and instrumental understanding. *Mathematical Teaching*, 77: 20–26.

Thomson, A. and Sylvester, R. (2010) Pupils to learn poetry by heart in Tory 'traditionalist' lesson plan for schools. *The Times*, 6 March, page 3.

2. The rapid recall of number facts

> ## Learning Outcomes
>
> By the end of this chapter you will:
> - understand what is meant by 'rapid recall of number facts' and its relationship with 'mental arithmetic';
> - know the curricular expectations with regard to the rapid recall of number facts;
> - be aware of a range of key principles related to the development of children's rapid recall of number facts.

Introduction

Rapid recall and mental arithmetic

For those who have a negative attitude towards mathematics, one of the first things that has to be done is convince them that the subject is not just about learning facts and rules. I'm sure that you have already been convinced of this by the research focus in Chapter 1 and so no further attempt will be made here to discuss the nature of mathematics. However, it is important to realise that in order to use mathematics effectively you do need to know some facts and be able to recall them instantly.

> ### Activity
> Here are three quick questions for you to answer. There's no need to write down the answers.
> 1. What is the capital city of France?
> 2. In which year did England win the football world cup?
> 3. Work out the sum of 5 and 3.

It's a fact – or is it?

Just in case you struggled with any of those, the answers are Paris, 1966 and 8. In most, if not all cases, you probably answered the question as soon as you read it. The answers are facts that you know and are able to recall mentally or verbally in an instant. The sum of 5 and 3 will certainly not be the only number fact that you know – there will be dozens, possibly hundreds of others that you could recall rapidly if required. But how did you acquire all of these facts? Knowing the number bonds to 10 and multiplication tables up to 10×10 is probably the result of experiences at school as a child, but your bank of known facts almost certainly extends beyond this. Perhaps you know, as a fact, that 13 squared is 169, or that pi is 3.142 to three decimal places, or that $\frac{3}{8}$ is 0.375 as a decimal. As you gain more experience of numbers and their relationships, your bank of known facts will grow. For example, over the years you may have calculated that 5 cubed is 125 so many times that you no longer need to work it out – you just know it as a fact!

Of course the boundary between knowing something as a fact and having to calculate an answer quickly is very blurred. I certainly know that $7 \times 8 = 56$ and that half of 48 is 24, but do I really know that 7 cubed is 343 and that $\frac{1}{11}$ is 0.090909, or did I need to work it out, albeit very rapidly? I'd like to think it was the former, but the important thing is that I am able to recall the answers very quickly as a result of my previous experience of working with these sorts of numbers. The same is true for you and for the children you teach. For 5-year-old children, it is the experience of adding 2 and 3 on many occasions, perhaps by using counters, then number lines and then wholly mentally, that eventually leads them to be able to recall the answer instantly as a fact, which they will know for the rest of their lives. For you, it might be your repeated experience of a dartboard which results in your knowing the doubles and triples of all the numbers up to 20. So the answers to many of the mental calculations we make today become the rapidly recalled number facts of tomorrow.

Distinguishing between known facts and mental arithmetic

Despite the blurred boundary between knowing number facts and calculating mentally, it is important to appreciate that there is a distinction between the two. For many people mental arithmetic is synonymous with the rapid recall of number facts, probably stemming from those uncomfortable childhood experiences when they were expected to respond instantly to a question from the teacher, or were given only a few seconds to jot down each answer in the weekly times tables or mental arithmetic test. Those sorts of experiences are clearly all about the rapid recall of number facts or knowing things 'off by heart', whereas mental arithmetic is the result of not knowing the answer and having to figure it out in your head. But you can only do this if you have access to relevant number facts that have previously been learned. For example, if you are mentally adding 27 and 34, and choose to do this by partitioning each of the numbers into tens and ones, you need to be able to calculate $20 + 30$ and $7 + 4$ efficiently in order to derive the final answer. Ideally $20 + 30$ and $7 + 4$ are known facts, but if they are not, this will increase the complexity of the calculation for you, reduce the efficiency of your method and increase the likelihood of getting the answer wrong. So if you have only a small bank of known facts and therefore rely on simple techniques such as counting on when working out $7 + 4$, this will severely restrict your ability to calculate mentally.

It is hoped that this discussion has clarified the distinction between the rapid recall of number facts and mental arithmetic, as well as the cyclical nature of their relationship. The answers to simple mental calculations eventually become known facts, which can then be used as the basis of more complex calculations. Over time, the answers to these calculations will become part of our ever-expanding bank of number facts, which will allow us to tackle increasingly complex problems. However, it is not the facts alone which allow us to carry out arithmetic effectively; these have to be combined with an understanding of how our number system works, often referred to as 'number sense' or having a 'feel for number'. This encompasses many things, including understanding the commutative, associative and distributive laws, appreciating the patterns within and relationships between numbers, and having an awareness of the relationships between the four arithmetical operations. These things will be explored in the next chapter when considering mental arithmetic.

Research Focus

Askew and William (1995) present evidence to indicate that children who are able to recall number facts, but are also able to use their deduction skills to work out things they cannot recall, make more progress than those who have access to only one approach. This is because each approach supports the other. The authors also consider the issue of children relying too heavily on counting to solve arithmetical problems, rather than developing a knowledge of number facts. Despite being able to use counting techniques to produce correct answers, this over-dependence removes the need to learn number facts, which in turn restricts children's ability to develop deductive approaches.

Both of these issues are also discussed by Gray (2008, page 87) who states that the child who has progressed from relying on counting techniques to knowing facts *possesses a powerful tool with which to achieve success in arithmetic* and goes on to say that *those who know facts and use them flexibly find arithmetic far easier than those who have to carry out counting procedures.*

What do children need to know?

Since the introduction of the National Curriculum in 1989 there has been a fairly consistent requirement set out in the programmes of study with regard to what children should be able to recall rapidly by the time they leave primary school. For example, the 1989 National Curriculum (DES, 1989) stated that children should be able to recall:

- addition and subtraction facts up to 10 (level 2);
- addition and subtraction facts up to 20 (level 3);
- multiplication facts for 2, 3, 4, 5 and 10 (level 3);
- multiplication facts up to 10×10 (level 4).

Although there was no requirement to rapidly recall division facts, children were expected to *derive quickly* the corresponding division facts for the multiplication facts up to 10×10.

The Primary Framework for Mathematics (DfES, 2006) did not have any additional requirements for rapid recall, although the expression 'derive' is used in the key learning objectives on a number of occasions, for example:

- derive sums and differences of pairs of multiples of 10, 100 or 1000;
- derive sums and differences and doubles and halves of decimals;

- derive related multiplication and division facts involving decimals.

As discussed in Chapter 1, the government has given some indication of its current priorities for arithmetic, one of which is as follows.

> *Children must be able to recall quickly and accurately basic 'number facts'*
> *(e.g. number bonds and multiplication tables).*

(DfE, 2012a)

This was followed in June 2012 by the publication of draft programmes of study for mathematics (DfE, 2012b) which state that children should be taught to:

- recall and use number bonds and related subtraction facts within 20 (Year 1);
- rapidly recall and use addition and subtraction facts to 20 (Year 2);
- recall multiplication and division facts for the 2, 5 and 10 multiplication tables (Year 2);
- recall and use multiplication and division facts for the 2, 3, 4, 5, 8 and 10 multiplication tables (Year 3);
- recall multiplication and division facts for multiplication tables up to 12×12 (Year 4).

These proposals do not represent a significant change in terms of what is expected of primary age children (apart from multiplication tables up to 12×12 being specified), but children are expected to do these things at an earlier age. For example, knowing all multiplication facts is currently a level 4 expectation, which is what we would expect the majority of children to be able to do by the time they leave primary school. In contrast, the draft proposals expect children to know multiplication facts up to 12×12 by the end of Year 4. It remains to be seen what the final programmes of study for mathematics will specify.

Given the vital role of rapid recall in the development of arithmetical competence, whatever statutory requirements are in place, they should be seen as a minimum expectation for many children. As discussed earlier in this chapter, it is hoped that many children will, with considerable encouragement from their teachers, expand their banks of number facts to include much more than addition and subtraction facts to 20 and multiplication facts up to 10×10.

Developing the rapid recall of number facts

Broad principles

When developing children's knowledge of number facts, the following key principles should be considered.

- Regular practice is required for children of all ages. A little bit of practice at frequent intervals is probably better than longer, infrequent activities.
- A variety of activities and approaches should be utilised to maintain the children's interest and to appeal to a range of preferred learning styles.

- Practical apparatus and visual aids are essential, incorporating the use of ICT where appropriate.
- An atmosphere should be cultivated in the classroom which promotes the learning of number facts as something positive and enjoyable, rather than something to fear.

> ### Activity
>
> Bearing in mind the key principles listed above, think about the ways that you have seen teachers developing and practising children's rapid recall of number facts. Try to identify specific examples of good practice that you have seen in school. If your school experience is limited at the moment, list examples of what you would consider to be good practice.
>
> When you've reflected on your experiences, compare your list with the guidance provided below.

Implications for your teaching

The following discussion is offered as general guidance for you to consider when providing opportunities for children to develop their recall of number facts.

The curriculum and beyond

A key consideration is to provide children with opportunities to practise and rehearse the recall of number facts regularly. This does not have to be at the start of every mathematics lesson – it might be at other times of the day and not necessarily as part of mathematics. Use a variety of approaches and activities, exploiting opportunities to work with individuals, pairs and small groups, as well as the whole class.

There are many ideas and resources available in school or online to help you plan for children to learn their number facts, for example the National Strategies' 'Springboard' and 'Wave 3' materials.

However, don't interpret the curriculum requirements in a narrow or literal way. So if children can recall their number bonds for 10 or 20, vary this to then look at number bonds for 15 or to 24. Similarly, when using counting on and counting back activities, don't always start at an exact multiple. So, for example, ask children to count on in 10s starting at 3, instead of always starting at zero or 10.

Remember, the recall of number facts is relevant not only to children in Key Stage 1 and lower Key Stage 2. All children should be constantly expanding their range of known number facts through regular consolidation and practice. Also encourage parents to be involved in their children's learning by providing homework activities which involve the rapid recall of number facts.

Resources

Resources are essential to support children's early learning of number facts. Use hundred squares, number lines, bead strings, counting sticks, a coat hanger and pegs, the children's fingers and so on to help develop children's flexible mental models and images. Particularly with young children, create visual displays to represent the number facts that you want them to learn. For example, representations of pairs that make 10, with the corresponding number sentence displayed under each one, will provide constant reinforcement for the children.

Resources also offer a way to vary your teaching approach. Provide a range of games and activities for the children to participate in, for example dice games, number track games, domino games, bingo, 'follow me' cards and so on. These provide children with a welcome alternative to simply responding to your quick-fire questions. Make use of songs, rhymes and chanting activities to help children to learn their number facts. Exploit the vast range of effective ICT resources that is available, often free of charge via the internet, for example the National Strategies' Interactive Teaching Programs. Use 'drill and practice' software creatively. These programs are designed for individual children to use sitting at the computer, but you can adapt their use for whole-class situations with the children using number fans or mini-whiteboards to provide their answers.

Questioning

Present questions in a variety of ways, for example orally, or on flash-cards, or on the interactive whiteboard, or using physical objects, and present number facts in unusual ways. So, for example, instead of relying on questions such as '7 + 9 =' use missing numbers such as '7 + □ = 16'. Also remember to use open as well as closed questions. So, for example, as an alternative to asking 'What is 3 multiplied by 8?' say 'Give me two numbers with a product of 24.'

When working with the whole class, encourage everyone to participate by giving the children access to number fans, digit cards or mini-whiteboards. Encourage young children to give their answers using complete number sentences, not just the answer, so as to reinforce key vocabulary.

Extending children's learning

Extend your discussions with the children to include tips on how to learn their number facts and show them how to use what they already know to work out new facts. However, don't rely simply on recalling facts – also give pupils opportunities to use and apply what they know and try to give a context to what you are doing. When you are discussing number facts, try to highlight and explain the relationships between operations, for example, by asking for a subtraction that corresponds to a given addition. Do take advantage of opportunities to highlight the characteristics of particular operations, for example the commutative property of addition and multiplication.

Case Study: Patterns in the multiplication tables

One of the key learning objectives for Kirsten's Year 4 class this term is to learn the multiplication facts for the 3s, 4s and 6s. Every day she fills spare moments with quick-fire practice and consequently the children are fairly competent with those multiplication facts, but in this particular mathematics lesson she wants to use the children's existing knowledge to explore patterns and connections.

She starts by asking the children to chant their multiples of 3, first forwards, then backwards. Then she displays the first ten multiples of 3 on the screen and asks the children to discuss in pairs anything interesting about the sequence of numbers. As she walks among the children she detects that they are struggling to find anything worthwhile to discuss and so provides a prompt:

Kirsten: Look out for odd numbers and even numbers. What do you notice?

This prompt generates much discussion which Kirsten follows up with the whole class.

Kirsten: So who can tell me anything they've spotted?

Alex: It goes odd, even, odd, even.

Kirsten: Well done, Alex. Can everyone see that? Do you think it will continue like that if we extend the sequence?

The children agree that it would and Kirsten discusses a few examples of this, beyond the 10th multiple on the screen. Then she puts a circle around each of the even multiples of 3 and asks the children what they can tell her about these.

Ben: They're all even numbers, Miss.

Kirsten: OK, thanks, Ben, but is there anything else? Where have you seen these numbers before?

Meg: It's the 6 times table – 6, 12, 18.

Kirsten: Excellent, Meg! Are we getting all of the numbers in the 6 times table or are there any missing?

The children conclude that all of the multiples of 6 are there and they also discuss the fact that if the sequence of multiples of 3 was continued, all of the other multiples of 6 would be there as well.

Kirsten: So what does that tell us about multiples of 6?

$\rightarrow$

Darren: They're all even.

Kirsten: Can anyone think of a multiple of 6 that isn't even? (No responses) OK, you're right – they're all even, but what else do we know?

Jenny: They're in the 3 times table.

Kirsten: Well done, Jenny, but how do you know that they're always going to be in the 3 times table?

Jenny: Well, if you've got 6 that means you've got 2 lots of 3, so it must be in the 3s.

This case study illustrates the importance of extending children's learning beyond the memorising of number facts, such as multiplication tables. Children need to understand the patterns and relationships that exist within and between these facts, but this is only going to happen if you provide the right sorts of opportunities for discussion.

Developing your own recall of number facts

As a trainee teacher, it is vitally important that you are able to recall number facts rapidly. You should be able to exceed the expectations of primary-aged children so as to equip yourself to use a range of mental and pencil and paper techniques.

Activity

Think about the list below and to what extent you can rapidly recall facts involving things such as:

- doubling and halving of whole numbers beyond 20, for example, half of 64;
- addition and subtraction of simple decimals and fractions, for example, $\frac{1}{2} + \frac{1}{4}$;
- equivalences between common fractions, decimals and percentages, for example, $\frac{3}{5}$, 60% and 0.6;
- simple fractional and percentage parts, for example, 25% of £80;
- special sets of numbers, for example, multiples, square numbers, factors, primes.

The list in the task above is not meant to be exhaustive – it includes just a few examples to illustrate how many useful number facts you can acquire, either naturally through simply working with these sorts of numbers, or in a more deliberate way involving regular practice. As discussed earlier in this chapter, the boundary between instant recall and rapid calculation is a blurred one, but the important thing is that you can access these facts quickly to help you carry out more complex tasks efficiently. So go on, push yourself and see how many number facts you can add to your existing bank – it really will empower you mathematically!

2 The rapid recall of number facts

> ## Learning Outcomes Review
>
> In order to carry out mental and pencil and paper arithmetic, such as those methods discussed in the next three chapters, it is vital that you have a bank of number facts at your disposal. Without these facts, other arithmetical methods will become cumbersome and inefficient. As a bare minimum, children should know their addition and subtraction facts up to 20 and their multiplication facts up to 10 × 10, but they should be encouraged to expand their bank of facts beyond this. If children rely on counting as an alternative to recalling number facts they will not be able to make the necessary progress in arithmetic. It is also important that the distinction between the rapid recall of number facts and the ability to calculate mentally is understood by teachers.

Further Reading

Thompson, I. (2008) 'From Counting to deriving number facts' in Thompson, I. (ed.) *Teaching and Learning Early Number*. Maidenhead: Open University Press.

References

Askew, W. and Wiliam, D. (1995) *Recent Research in Mathematics Education 5–16*. London: Ofsted.

DES (1989) *Mathematics in the National Curriculum*. London: HMSO.

DfE (2012a) *Key priorities for arithmetic*. Presentation to ITT mathematics tutors, TDA/UCET/ NASBTT conference for Primary ITT tutors, Lancaster and London. March, 2012.

DfE (2012b) *National Curriculum for Mathematics: Key Stages 1 and 2 – Draft*. London: DfE Publications.

DfES (2006) *Primary Framework for Literacy and Mathematics*. Available at: www.niched.org/ docs/the%20primary%20framework.pdf (accessed June 2012).

Gray, E. (2008) Compressing the counting process: strength from the flexible interpretation of symbols, in Thompson, I. (ed.) *Teaching and Learning Early Number*. Maidenhead: Open University Press.

3. Mental arithmetic

Learning Outcomes
....

By the end of this chapter you will:
- be aware of a wide range of mental calculation strategies involving the addition, subtraction, multiplication and division of whole numbers;
- understand the mathematical laws and principles which underpin mental calculation;
- appreciate that an understanding of place value and the relationships between operations is vitally important when developing mental calculation strategies.

Introduction

The status of mental methods

As discussed already in this book, being able to calculate mentally should be viewed as a vitally important component of every person's mathematical capability. Indeed, it is important that children view mental methods as always being the first resort. Whenever faced with a calculation they should always ask the question 'Can I do it mentally?' Cultivating this sort of positive attitude towards mental methods can only be achieved by teaching them in a carefully planned, structured way, which will require a considerable investment of time. Consequently, mental mathematics should not be restricted to oral-mental starters at the beginning of lessons, because these short sessions tend to focus on the practising and refining of existing skills rather than teaching new ones. A key recommendation of the Williams Review (DCSF, 2008) was *a renewed focus on oral and mental mathematics* (page 60), but this should not be interpreted solely in the form of more oral-mental starters. A more careful examination of the review reveals that it is the role and status of mental mathematics in the broadest sense that requires a greater focus as well as its relationship with pencil and paper approaches. So if you want to give mental mathematics the high status recommended by Williams, and are going to be teaching all of the techniques and approaches suggested in this chapter, you will need to set aside the main parts of a substantial number of mathematics lessons to do this – ten minutes at the start of a lesson will not be sufficient.

Mental methods should also be afforded high status beyond mathematics lessons by continually providing children with opportunities to practise and utilise their calculating skills throughout the day (see Hansen and Vaukins, 2011, for further discussion about cross-curricular mathematics). Developing mental agility across the curriculum will not only serve children well in their everyday lives, but will also equip them to access, explore and understand other aspects of mathematics more effectively, for example the use of written methods of calculation, as we shall see in Chapter 4. It is also worth emphasising that when children start to use pencil and paper approaches this should not result in a lowering of the status of mental calculation strategies. Therefore, as children get older they should be constantly expanding the range and types of numbers they can work with mentally and continue to view mental methods as the first resort when faced with any calculation.

The importance of discussion

Williams (DCSF, 2008) highlighted the importance of high quality talk in mathematics and this is of particular relevance to the development of mental calculation strategies. It is important to encourage children to explain, share, compare and contrast the mental methods that they are using, making use of appropriate co-operative learning techniques such as 'talk partners', 'think-pair-share' and so on. Many teachers are very comfortable using these sorts of techniques to encourage speaking and listening as part of literacy lessons, or more widely across the curriculum, but not always to the same extent in mathematics. Perhaps this is because discussion-based lessons, which focus on the development of mental calculation strategies, result in children having little or nothing written in their books. The absence of written 'evidence' in an exercise book or on a worksheet does not mean the children have learned nothing, so it is not an issue to be unduly concerned about.

The key message, then, is to actively promote discussion in mathematics in the same way as in other aspects of the curriculum. One particular way of doing this is to use a child's error or inefficient mental strategy as an opportunity to introduce a more efficient one, possibly suggested by one of the other children. Not only does this develop children's understanding, it also creates an ethos in the classroom which encourages the children to 'have a go' and not to fear making a mistake or using the 'wrong' method. The ultimate aim is to build up the children's confidence as well as their ability, so that they feel comfortable using mental methods and talking about mathematics.

In order to support children's ability to talk about mathematics you should plan for the use of appropriate models and images. Resources such as 100 squares, number lines, bead strings, arrays, partitioning cards, etc. support the children's development of mental calculation strategies by offering a picture in their minds that they can use.

Another issue to be aware of is that because calculating mentally is not the same as instant recall it is important that you give children time to think and to formulate their responses. This issue was raised in the Williams Review which states that:

> the review panel have observed numerous examples of undue haste on the part of practitioners during their discussions with children – in some cases even delivering the answers to their own questions before the child has had time to formulate his or her thoughts.

> (DCSF, 2008, page 64)

Even if you do give children sufficient 'thinking time' you also need to be mindful of the fact that those children who work out the answers quickly, and so thrust their hands into the air, can intimidate those who are still thinking, so perhaps make use of 'no hands' approaches or something similar.

The approach adopted for a large part of this chapter is to get you to engage in a variety of mental calculations and then to use these as a vehicle to explore a wide range of strategies that can be used. This approach has the dual purpose of addressing your own subject knowledge, that is, your ability to calculate mentally, while at the same time developing your pedagogical understanding of what you will need to teach children. Although pairs of operations are considered separately in this chapter, it is important that you constantly remind children of the relationships between the four operations so that they do not view each one as a separate entity. What we do not want is a child who sees a number sentence involving subtraction to only ever think in terms of 'taking away' or counting backwards.

Mental calculation strategies for addition and subtraction

Remember, it is important to ensure that children have the prerequisite knowledge of number facts, to equip them to calculate mentally. Mental calculation strategies can start to be developed with a relatively small bank of known number facts, but it is important that this bank is expanded through regular practice, as discussed in Chapter 2.

Activity

Try to mentally work out the answer to each of the questions below. You must not write down anything other than the answer and you must not use a calculator.
When you have written down your answers, think carefully about how you tackled each question and make brief notes which explain the method you used.

1. $75 - 23$
2. $57 + 39$
3. $83 - 57$
4. $28 + 16 + 14$
5. $64 - 37 - 23$
6. $502 - 496$

Here are some possible ways that each of the questions could have been answered. Your approaches, or something similar, might be among those listed. Read the possibilities carefully and make sure you understand what is being explained in each case.

Question 1: 75 − 23
- Visualise the traditional pencil and paper method, with 75 above 23, in columns, and the answer (52) written underneath.

- Partition the two numbers and then work out 70 − 20 = 50 and 5 − 3 = 2. Would it matter which calculation you do first?
- Round 23 up to 25, subtract 25 from 75 (50) and add 2 to compensate for the original rounding up.
- Subtract 20 from 75 (55) and then subtract 3 from 55, or alternatively subtract 3, then 20.
- Count back from 75 until you get to 23, probably in stages, for example 75 down to 25 (50) and then down 2 more to 23.
- Count up from 23 to 75, probably in stages, for example 23 to 30 (7), 30 to 70 (40) and 70 to 75 (5), or alternatively 23 to 73 (50) and 73 to 75 (2).

Question 2: 57 + 39

- Visualise the traditional pencil and paper method, with 57 above 39, in columns, and the answer (96) written underneath. Would you be able to manage the 'carrying'?
- Partition the two numbers and then work out 50 + 30 = 80 and 7 + 9 = 16. Would it matter which calculation you do first?
- Round 39 up to 40, adding this to 57 (97) and subtract 1 to compensate for the original rounding up.
- Add 30 to 57 (87) and then add 9, or alternatively add 9, then 30.
- Add 33 to 57 (90 – but why might you do it this way?) and then add 6.

Question 3: 83 − 57

- Visualise the traditional pencil and paper method, with 83 above 57, in columns, and the answer (26) written underneath. Would you be able to manage the 'borrowing'?
- Round 57 up to 60, subtract 60 from 83 (23) and add 3 to compensate for the original rounding up.
- Subtract 50 from 83 (33) and then subtract 7 from 33, or alternatively subtract 7, then 50.
- Count back from 83 until you get to 57, probably in stages, for example 83 down to 63 (20) and then down 6 more to 57.
- Count up from 57 to 83, probably in stages, for example 57 to 60 (3), 60 to 80 (20) and 80 to 83 (3), or alternatively 57 to 77 (20) and 77 to 83 (6).

Question 4: 28 + 16 + 14

- Visualise the traditional pencil and paper method, with the three numbers in columns, and the answer (58) written underneath. Would you be able to manage the 'carrying'?
- Partition the three numbers and then work out 20 + 10 + 10 = 40 and 8 + 6 + 4 = 18. (Would you add the single-digit numbers in the order in which they appear?)

- Add the numbers as they appear from left to right, i.e. 28 + 16 = 44 (which can be done in a variety of ways) and then 44 + 14 = 58.

- Look along the list to find numbers that go together and so can be added quickly, i.e. 16 + 14 = 30, and then add 28.

Question 5: 64 − 37 − 23

- Working from left to right, calculate 64 − 37 = 27 (which can be done in a variety of ways) and then 27 − 23 = 4.

- Subtract 23 from 64 (41) and then subtract 37 (4). Why might it be easier to do the subtractions in this order?

- Make use of the fact that subtracting 37 and then subtracting 23 is equivalent to subtracting the sum of these two numbers, and also the fact that they can be added quickly to give 60. Finally, 64 − 60 = 4.

Question 6: 502 − 496

- Visualise the traditional pencil and paper method, with 502 above 496, in columns, and the answer (6) written underneath. Would you be able to manage the 'borrowing'?

- Recognise that the two numbers, despite being quite large, are very close together and so count on from 496 to 502 or count back from 502 to 496.

Efficient mental calculating strategies for addition and subtraction

There is no suggestion that the approaches listed above are equally efficient. Some are more efficient than others and it is important for you, as a teacher, to be aware of efficient and inefficient strategies.

Activity

For each of the six addition and subtraction questions presented and discussed above, identify the mental calculation strategy which is, in your opinion, the most efficient one to use. Also try to identify the one which is the most inefficient.

If you were to compare your views about efficient strategies with those of a colleague, you would not necessarily agree. This highlights an important feature of mental calculation strategies, that is, they are very personal and idiosyncratic. What works well for one person may be considered bizarre by another. Having said that, it is hoped that you do not consider the visualisation of traditional pencil and paper arithmetic to be a realistic approach to mental calculation. If you do, it is vitally important that you open your mind to the alternatives because there is certainly a more efficient approach available.

The efficient approaches utilised in answering the six questions above are based on techniques such as:

- partitioning the digits into tens and ones, or hundreds, tens and ones;
- counting up from the lower number to the higher, recognising the relationship between addition and subtraction;
- rounding to the nearest multiple of 10 and then adjusting the answer;
- looking along a list of numbers to see which ones can be combined efficiently.

In the next section you will be able to utilise these techniques again to tackle mental multiplications and divisions, and you will also be introduced to some additional techniques to add to your repertoire.

Mental calculation strategies for multiplication and division

Activity

Try to mentally work out the answer to each of the questions below. You must not write down anything other than the answer and you must not use a calculator.

When you have written down your answers, think carefully about how you tackled each question and make brief notes which explain the method you used.

1. 14×8
2. 5×39
3. $2 \times 9 \times 6 \times 5$
4. $188 \div 4$
5. 25×17
6. $340 \div 5$

Question 1: 14×8

- Visualise the traditional pencil and paper method, with 14 above 8, in columns, and the answer (112) written underneath. Would you be able to manage the 'carrying'?
- Partition 14 and then work out $10 \times 8 = 80$ and $4 \times 8 = 32$. Would it matter which calculation you do first?
- Round 8 up to 10, work out 14×10 (140) and then subtract two lots of 14 (28) to compensate for the original rounding up.
- Use repeated doubling of 14, i.e. 14, 28, 56, 112.

Question 2: 5×39

- Visualise the traditional pencil and paper method, with 39 above 5, in columns, and the answer (195) written underneath. Would you be able to manage the 'carrying'?

- Partition 39 and then work out $30 \times 5 = 150$ and $9 \times 5 = 45$ and finally add these two answers. Would it matter which calculation you do first?
- Round 39 up to 40, work out 40×5 (200) and then subtract one lot of 5 to compensate for the original rounding up.
- Multiply 39 by 10 (390) and then halve the answer to give 195.

Question 3: $2 \times 9 \times 6 \times 5$

- Multiply the numbers as they appear from left to right, i.e. $2 \times 9 = 18$, $18 \times 6 = 108$, $108 \times 5 = 540$. (How might you do these last two calculations?)
- Look along the list to find numbers that can be multiplied together quickly and also provide answers that make subsequent calculations easier, i.e. work out $2 \times 5 = 10$, then work out $9 \times 6 = 54$ and finally work out $54 \times 10 = 540$.

Question 3: $188 \div 4$

- Visualise the traditional pencil and paper method, using the division 'bracket' and with any remainders squeezed in front of the next digit.
- Partition 188 into 100, 80 and 8, then divide each of these by 4 and finally add the three answers (25, 20 and 2) together.
- Round 188 up to 200, divide 200 by 4 (50) and then subtract one quarter of the amount you rounded up (i.e. a quarter of 12).
- Use repeated halving, i.e. half of 188 is 94 and half of 94 is 47. (How might you do these two calculations?)
- Make use of the fact that $4 \times 40 = 160$. This is 28 less than 188, so 28 must be divided by 4 (7) and then added to the 40 to give 47. Essentially, this method involves partitioning 188 into 160 and 28.

Question 5: 25×17

- Visualise the traditional pencil and paper method, with 25 above 17, in columns, and the answer (425) written underneath.
- Partition 25 and then work out $20 \times 17 = 340$ and $5 \times 17 = 85$. Finally, add these two answers.
- Partition 17 and then work out $10 \times 25 = 250$ and $7 \times 25 = 175$. Finally, add these two answers.
- Round 17 up to 20, work out 20×25 (500) and then subtract three lots of 25 (75) to compensate for the original rounding up.
- Make use of the fact that every four lots of 25 is 100, so in 17 lots there will be four 100s and one lot of 25 left over.

- Recognise that multiplying by 25 is equivalent to multiplying by 100 and dividing by 4 (because every lot of 100 contains 4 lots of 25). So $17 \times 100 = 1700$ and $1700 \div 4 = 425$. (How might you divide by 4?) The two stages could be done in reverse, that is, divide 17 by 4 (4.25) and then multiply by 100 (425).

Question 6: 340 ÷ 5

- Visualise the traditional pencil and paper method, using the division 'bracket' and with any remainders squeezed in front of the next digit.
- Partition 340 into 300 and 40, then divide each of these by 5 and finally add the two answers (60 and 8) together.
- Recognise that dividing by 5 is equivalent to dividing by 10 and then doubling the answer (because for every lot of 10 there are two lots of 5). So $340 \div 10 = 34$ and $34 \times 2 = 68$.

Efficient mental calculating strategies for multiplication and division

As was the case with the addition and subtraction discussed earlier in this chapter, some approaches are more efficient than others. It is important that you are able to quickly evaluate these, so as to identify efficient and inefficient mental calculation strategies.

> ### Activity
> For each of the six multiplication and division questions presented and discussed above, identify the mental calculation strategy which is, in your opinion, the most efficient one to use. Also try to identify the one which is the most inefficient.

Again, there is no suggestion that there is a 'correct' or 'best' approach, but you should have concluded that visualising traditional pencil and paper methods is not as efficient as the alternative methods. It is also hoped that you are employing mental strategies which make use of things such as near multiples of 10; the relationships between operations; partitioning into hundreds, tens and ones; and combining numbers not necessarily in the order in which they are listed. These techniques were identified earlier in relation to mental addition and subtraction, but they can also be applied to mental multiplication and division, as demonstrated above. Additionally, the following techniques have also been exemplified.

- The use of repeated doubling for multiplication by 4, 8, 16, etc. This is an example of using factors, that is, when multiplying by 8, you break it down into the factors 2, 2 and 2 and multiply by each of these. This technique can be applied in other ways, for example multiplication by 12 can be achieved by multiplying by 3 followed by 4, because 3 and 4 are a factor pair for 12.
- The use of repeated halving for division by 4, 8, 16, etc. As with repeated multiplication, this use of factors can be applied in other ways, for example division by 6 can be achieved by halving and then dividing by 3, because 2 and 3 are a factor pair for 6.

- The use of equivalent calculation combinations, for example using multiplication by 10 and halving as an equivalent to multiplication by 5, or using multiplication by 100 and division by 4 as an equivalent to multiplication by 25.

As well as employing these sorts of techniques, the mental calculations considered above require an understanding of place value as well as the commutative, distributive and associative laws of arithmetic. If the mental approaches you were using earlier have been effective and efficient, then clearly you must possess a good understanding of these laws, even if you are not aware of it! Just in case you are not fully conversant with the laws of arithmetic or the different ways of considering place value, further explanation is provided in the following sections.

In your teaching, having examined a wide range of mental techniques for addition, subtraction, multiplication and division in the sections above, it is important that you plan and teach appropriate lessons which focus on these methods, based on partitioning, near multiples of 10, repeated doubling and halving and so on, so that your children can develop high levels of mental agility.

Place value: 'column value' or 'quantity value'

An understanding of place value, like the recall of number facts, is essential for mental calculation strategies and so is required from the outset. It is important that you do not make the mistake of thinking that place value is something that is taught and practised only in Key Stage 1. As children encounter bigger numbers and different types of numbers, such as decimals, their knowledge of place value will have to be extended.

The vast majority of the mental calculation strategies discussed above are based upon a firm understanding of the concept of place value and the ability to employ the technique of partitioning. So, for example, when calculating $75 - 23$ you may have partitioned 75 into 20 and 5 and partitioned 23 into 20 and 3. Here you are using the notion of 'quantity value' because you view the 7 as 70, as opposed to viewing it as '7 tens' or '7 in the tens column', which is often the way that place value is introduced to young children. When carrying out mental calculations the 'quantity value' approach would appear to be the better way of viewing the concept of place value because it enables you to manipulate the actual numbers that the individual digits represent.

Research Focus 'Column value' and 'quantity value'

Thompson (2009) and Thompson and Bramald (2002) provide a more detailed discussion of the 'column value' and 'quantity value' aspects of place value. They also consider historical perspectives in terms of the ways that young children have traditionally been introduced to place value and how this relates to the development of mental and written calculation skills. They argue that the traditional definition of place value, which would explain the number 43 as '4 in

$\longrightarrow$

the tens column' or '4 lots of 10', is an outdated one and does not reflect the way that children actually carry out mental calculations. So, for example, when adding 43 and 52, most people would think in terms of '40 plus 50' and '3 plus 2', that is, 'quantity value' rather than 'column value'. The authors provide similar examples involving subtraction, multiplication and division and also demonstrate how 'quantity value' underpins informal pencil and paper arithmetic (which is considered in Chapter 4 of this book). It is only the traditional pencil and paper methods that utilise 'column value'.

The laws of arithmetic

The commutative law

You intuitively understand the commutative law whenever you add, subtract, multiply or divide two numbers, because you know that sometimes it is possible to switch the numbers, but on other occasions you cannot. For example, if partitioning is used to calculate $34 + 52$, the intermediate answers (80 and 6) can be added in either order, because $80 + 6 = 6 + 80 = 86$. Similarly, when calculating the product of 5 and 19 you can think of it as 5×19 or 19×5 because the answer will be the same. You can do this switching because both addition and multiplication are commutative. Subtraction and division however, are not commutative, as illustrated below.

$12 - 4 = 8$ whereas $4 - 12 = -8$

$10 \div 2 = 5$ whereas $2 \div 10 = 0.2$

The distributive law

If you used partitioning when you calculated 14×8 earlier, you certainly understand the distributive law. You know that 14 lots of 8 is equivalent to 10 lots of 8 plus 4 lots of 8. This is because multiplication by 8 can be distributed over the addition of 10 and 4. In formal notation this can be written as:

14×8 $= 8 \times 14$ (the commutative law)

                  $= 8 \times (10 + 4)$ (partitioning)

                  $= 8 \times 10 + 8 \times 4$ (multiplication distributed over addition)

                  $= 80 + 32$

                  $= 112$

Earlier you may have used near multiples of 10 to calculate 5×39, which again demonstrates your understanding of the distributive law. You know that 39 lots of 5 is equivalent to 40 lots of 5 minus 1 lot of 5. This is because multiplication by 5 can be distributed over the subtraction of 1 from 40, as explained below.

$$5 \times 39 \qquad = 5 \times (40 - 1)$$
$$= 5 \times 40 - 5 \times 1 \text{ (multiplication distributed over subtraction)}$$
$$= 200 - 5$$
$$= 195$$

Division can be distributed over both addition and subtraction, as illustrated by the examples below, which consider two of the ways of calculating $188 \div 4$ that were discussed earlier.

Method 1: Think of 188 as being $200 - 12$ and divide each of these by 4.

$$188 \div 4 \qquad = (200 - 12) \div 4$$
$$= 200 \div 4 - 12 \div 4 \text{ (division distributed over subtraction)}$$
$$= 50 - 3$$
$$= 47$$

Method 2: Think of 188 as being $160 + 28$ and divide each of these by 4.

$$188 \div 4 \qquad = (160 + 28) \div 4$$
$$= 160 \div 4 + 28 \div 4 \text{ (division distributed over addition)}$$
$$= 40 + 7$$
$$= 47$$

The associative law

This can be thought of as an extension of the commutative law because it relates to the order in which we combine three or more numbers. You may have demonstrated an understanding of the associative law earlier when calculating $28 + 16 + 14$ and $2 \times 9 \times 6 \times 5$. In the first question you possibly worked out $16 + 14$ first, and then added 28. You can do this because addition is associative. Similarly, in the second question you can change the order in which the numbers are combined because multiplication is associative.

Earlier, the way that you calculated $64 - 37 - 23$ probably demonstrates that you know that subtraction is not associative, as illustrated below, by using brackets to indicate the different orders in which the subtractions are being carried out.

$$(64 - 37) - 23 \quad = 27 - 23$$
$$= 4 \qquad \text{(which is the correct answer to the original question)}$$
$$64 - (37 - 23) \quad = 64 - 14$$
$$= 50 \qquad \text{(which is } not \text{ the correct answer to the original question)}$$

Similarly, division is not associative, as illustrated by the following example:

$(8 \div 4) \div 2 \qquad = 2 \div 2$

$\qquad\qquad\qquad = 1$

whereas

$8 \div (4 \div 2) \qquad = 8 \div 2$

$\qquad\qquad\qquad = 4$

It is not necessary for children to know these laws by name or to be taught them in a formal way. What is important, however, is that they are able to demonstrate an understanding of them when they carry out calculations, in the ways that have been discussed throughout this chapter. In essence what is required is an understanding of how the four operations can be combined, either singly or with one another, in different ways to produce alternative, but equivalent, number sentences which result in correct answers.

Case Study

Donna is a trainee teacher in a Year 6 class on her final placement. During an ICT lesson using LOGO, some of the children are trying to write a procedure to draw a regular dodecagon and so need to work out the angle through which the turtle would turn after each forward movement. Donna is encouraging the children to use their mental skills to calculate the answer to $360 \div 12$. Here is part of the dialogue between Donna and one of the children, Ben.

Donna: So what do you think, Ben?

Ben: 18, Miss.

Donna: How did you work it out?

Ben: Well, I partitioned the 12 into 10 and 2. So 360 divided by 10 is 36 and 36 divided by 2 is 18.

Donna: Erm ... That's a good try, Ben, but not quite right. Did anyone get a different answer?

Donna knows that the answer is wrong, but she does not know why. She is therefore unable to explain to Ben the flaw in his method.

Can you see where Ben has gone wrong?

Which law of arithmetic has he tried to apply, but incorrectly?

Ben has tried to use the distributive law but inappropriately. Division by a particular number (the 'divisor') can be distributed over addition or subtraction within the number being divided (the 'dividend') as illustrated by the example earlier:

$\rightarrow$

$$188 \div 4 = (160 + 28) \div 4$$

or

$$188 \div 4 = (200 - 12) \div 4$$

However, you cannot express the divisor as the sum or difference of two numbers and then divide by each one in turn.

Division can be distributed over both addition and subtraction, but it is the dividend that must be expressed as a sum or difference, and then each part divided by the divisor.

Equipping children to calculate mentally

If we want children to use efficient mental calculation strategies, then it is important that the appropriate foundations are laid. These foundations are presented below under three broad headings.

Recall of number facts

The ability to recall number facts is a key prerequisite for efficient mental calculation. As discussed in Chapter 2, if children are relying heavily on counting techniques as a substitute for the recall of number facts, this will limit their ability to calculate mentally.

Understanding the number system

This is often referred to as having a 'feel for number' or 'number sense'. It involves having a good understanding of number patterns and relationships, including an understanding of place value. Specific examples include understanding that:

• numbers ending with a zero are divisible by 10;

• all numbers ending in 0 or 5 are divisible by 5;

• all multiples of 2, 4, 6, 8, etc. are even;

• all multiples of 9 and 6 are also multiples of 3;

• alternate multiples of 3 are even and are also multiples of 6;

• a number that is divisible by 12 must be divisible by both 3 and 4.

It is also important to understand the nature of the four number operations, including their commutative, distributive and associative properties, as well as the way that they relate to one another. Specific examples of this include understanding:

• that when adding, increasing one number by a fixed amount and decreasing the other by the same amount will not affect the answer, for example 29 + 36 = 30 + 35 (add 1 to one number and subtract 1 from the other);

- that when subtracting, you can increase or decrease both numbers by the same amount and it will not affect the answer, for example $81 - 24 = 80 - 23$ (subtract 1 from both numbers);

- that when multiplying, you can multiply one number by a fixed amount and divide the other by the same amount and it will not affect the answer, for example $15 \times 18 = 3 \times 90$ (divide one number by 5 and multiply the other by 5);

- that when dividing, you can multiply or divide both numbers by the same amount and it will not affect the answer, for example $390 \div 15 = 39 \div 1.5 = 78 \div 3$ (divide both by 10, then multiply both by 2);

- the inverse relationship between addition and subtraction, so that, for example, a subtraction can be tackled by counting on from the lower number to the higher;

- the inverse relationship between multiplication and division, so that, for example, $480 \div 40$ can be thought of as 'What do I multiply 40 by to get 480?';

- multiplication as repeated addition;

- division as repeated subtraction;

- the 'oddness' or 'evenness' relationships when numbers are added, subtracted, multiplied and divided; e.g. if you multiply two odd numbers the product will be odd;

- the effects of adding, subtracting, multiplying and dividing by zero and 1.

Mental arithmetic techniques

Children need to be able to utilise their recall of number facts, in conjunction with their understanding of the number system, to employ a wide range of techniques to carry out efficient mental calculations. These are the sorts of techniques that were discussed earlier in this chapter, when you tackled six additions and subtractions and then six multiplications and divisions. Some children who can recall number facts and have a good 'feel for number' will be able to devise these techniques themselves, but the majority of children are not capable of this and so they have to be taught in a carefully planned, structured way.

Research Focus: A model of mental calculation

Thompson (2010) provides a historical perspective on the teaching of mental calculation and also presents a summary of key research in this area. He concludes by presenting a *model of mental calculation*, which comprises *facts* (for example addition and subtraction facts to 20, multiplication tables and corresponding division facts), *understandings* (what Thompson refers to as *number sense* and including the sorts of things outlined in the section above) and *skills* (for example counting on from the higher number when adding, rather than counting all of the objects). These three components of Thompson's model of mental calculation correspond closely to the three subheadings used above. Additionally, Thompson's

$\rightarrow$

model identifies *attitudes* as the fourth component of his model, that is, children's confidence in their ability to use mental strategies, which Thompson describes as *an important but neglected ingredient* (page 170). He states that a change of attitude to mental calculation is needed so that children are prepared to *have a go* and not simply say *I can't remember the method so I cannot solve the problem.*

Implications for your teaching

As stated above, it is important that mental calculation strategies are taught in a planned, structured way. To assist you with this, the following general guidelines are offered, some of which have been suggested already in this chapter.

The importance of counting

Counting activities form the basis of early calculation and help children to develop a 'feel for number' but, like place value, these should not be restricted to Key Stage 1. Older children can develop their understanding of the number system, and therefore their ability to calculate mentally, by engaging in activities such as: counting forwards and backwards in multiples of 3, 4, 5, etc; counting in multiples but not starting at an exact multiple; counting involving repeated doubling or halving; counting involving sequences such as square numbers; counting forwards and backwards in larger steps, to encourage mental calculation. So, for example, you could ask children in upper Key Stage 2 to chant the multiples of 17 – '17, 34, 51, 68, 85 ...' – and discuss the strategies they use to quickly work out each one. Discussion-based activities such as this result in nothing being written down, but nevertheless can result in much learning taking place. By employing co-operative learning techniques, like those suggested at the beginning of this chapter, it is also possible to involve all children in the discussions. There will also be opportunities to effectively utilise models and images, such as number lines, counting sticks, 100 squares, etc.

Using and applying mental skills

Like any other mathematical technique or skill, the whole point of developing and mastering efficient mental methods is to use them – you should not be teaching these things just for the sake of it. It is therefore vitally important that you provide appropriate opportunities for children to use and apply their mental skills in mathematics through problem-solving activities and open-ended, investigative tasks. The use and application of these skills should also extend right across the curriculum and throughout children's everyday lives.

Mental arithmetic – always the first resort

The status of mental mathematics has already been considered at the beginning of this chapter, but it is appropriate to reiterate this again here. Children of all ages as well as adults, should be constantly striving to develop and extend their mental capabilities, because these are essential skills for life. They never become redundant and should never be abandoned when pencil and paper methods are introduced, or when an electronic calculator becomes available; indeed they facilitate the effective development of these alternative approaches, as we shall see in Chapters 4 and 7. Children should be proud of their ability to mentally juggle with large numbers, negative numbers, fractions, decimals, percentages and anything else that their everyday lives throw up.

Learning Outcomes Review

You should now be aware of a wide range of strategies that can be utilised when carrying out mental arithmetic, as well as appreciate the vitally important role they play in equipping us all, children and adults, for our everyday lives. However, having 'awareness' is not sufficient – you need to be able to put these strategies into practice so that you are able to mentally juggle with numbers and calculate efficiently. If mental arithmetic is not one of your strengths (possibly because it was not given sufficient emphasis when you were a child at school) then you must spend time practising and developing your own skills, so that you can be a role model for the children you teach.

As well as knowing a range of strategies, you should understand the laws of arithmetic, the role of place value and the interrelated nature of the four arithmetical operations, and also appreciate how these underpin mental arithmetic.

In teaching mental arithmetic you should appreciate that children need to be secure in their knowledge of number facts, should have a good understanding of the number system and should be confident when working with numbers. Finally, they need to be taught all of the calculating techniques in a structured way because the majority of children are not capable of developing these for themselves.

Self assessment questions

1. If, when calculating 13×25, you partition 13 into 10 and 3 and then multiply each of these by 25, which of the laws of arithmetic are you basing your method on?
2. If, when calculating $17 \times 5 \times 2$, you work out 5×2 first and then multiply the answer by 17, which of the laws of arithmetic are you basing your method on?
3. Work out the answer to each of the following questions by using an efficient mental method. Make a note of the answer and the method you use.
   a. $135 \div 5$
   b. $38 + 26 + 26$
   c. $5004 - 1947$
   d. $33 \times 7 \times 3$

Further Reading

DfE (2010) *Teaching Children to Calculate Mentally*. London: DfE Publications.

Hansen, A. and Vaukins, D. (2011) *Primary Mathematics across the Curriculum*. London: Learning Matters. Read Chapter 2 ('Number') although other sections of the book will also be of general interest.

QCA (1999) *Teaching Mental Calculation Strategies: Guidance for teachers at Key Stages 1 and 2*. Sudbury: QCA Publications.

References

DCSF (2008) *Independent Review of Mathematics Teaching in Early Years Settings and Primary Schools* (The Williams Review). Nottingham: DCSF Publications.

Thompson, I. (2009) 'Place value?' *Mathematics Teaching*, 215: 4–5.

Thompson, I. (2010) Getting your head around mental calculation, in Thompson, I. (ed.) *Issues in Teaching Numeracy in Primary Schools*. Maidenhead: Open University Press.

Thompson, I. and Bramald, R. (2002) *An investigation of the relationship between young children's understanding of place value and their competence at mental addition*. Final report submitted to the Nuffield Foundation. Newcastle: Department of Education, University of Newcastle upon Tyne.

4. The development of pencil and paper arithmetic

Learning Outcomes

By the end of this chapter you will:

- appreciate that pencil and paper arithmetic evolves naturally from the mental calculation strategies considered in Chapter 3;
- be aware of a range of informal pencil and paper approaches, covering all four operations;
- appreciate the role and status of the informal methods discussed in this chapter;
- understand progression in the development of pencil and paper arithmetic, eventually working towards the introduction of the traditional algorithms presented in Chapter 5.

Introduction

Before the advent of the National Numeracy Strategy in 1999 it was common practice to introduce children to the traditional pencil and paper methods for addition, subtraction, multiplication and division as early as possible. Typically, in the case of addition and subtraction, this was at the age of 6 or 7, that is, as soon as children were able to mentally add and subtract two single-digit numbers. However, research has shown that this was not effective, with many children failing to understand what they were doing and often getting incorrect answers. The 1999 *Framework for Teaching Mathematics* (DfEE, 1999) provided clear lines of progression in the development of pencil and paper arithmetic during Key Stage 2 by presenting informal, expanded written methods based on the mental strategies that should have already been taught. The traditional pencil and paper methods were presented as being the final stage in this progression, instead of the initial one as had previously been the case. Even the most recent guidance from the National Strategies (2011) continued to support this model of progression in children's arithmetic, although the guidance did emphasise that the informal, expanded pencil and paper methods should be viewed as 'staging posts' on the way to more compact, efficient methods, rather than being end points in themselves.

In its deliberations over the development of the new mathematics National Curriculum for England, the Department for Education has expressed similar views. It has stated that:

- *Children must be fluent in applying quick, efficient written methods of calculation.*
- *Children need to be moved on rapidly to use appropriate efficient written methods,*

> rather than becoming dependent on intermediate methods. This should be reflected in school policy. No child should be labouring with interim calculation methods in the long term.

(DfE, 2012a)

The Department for Education has also acknowledged the important role of other aspects of teaching and learning arithmetic, stating that:

> Children need to understand and use the mathematical concepts that underpin number and arithmetic, such as place value. Without such concepts, pupils are ultimately less able to perform mental or written calculations, solve problems and reason mathematically.

> All children must leave primary school both proficient in the school's arithmetical algorithm for each operation and with a good understanding of the underpinning mathematics, both of which will equip them for solving unfamiliar problems and as a foundation for the more complex mathematics they will be taught in secondary school.

(DfE, 2012a)

More recently the government has published draft programmes of study for mathematics (DfE, 2012b) which, like the priorities presented above, do not explicitly afford as high a status to informal pencil and paper approaches as in the past. The draft proposals make some references to 'efficient' and 'reliable' written methods, and often they are simply referred to as 'written methods', possibly leaving the reader to interpret this in whatever way is appropriate. Only when the final versions of the programmes of study are published will we have a clearer understanding of the government's interpretation of what is meant by 'written methods'.

The first section of this chapter discusses some of the issues relating to the DfE priorities for arithmetic identified above and provides some suggestions for helping children to develop effective pencil and paper procedures. The remainder of this chapter will adopt a similar approach to the one in Chapter 3, that is, you will be asked to tackle a variety of questions using pencil and paper methods of your choice. These will be used as a vehicle to explore the full range of strategies that can be used, including lines of progression. This will address your own subject knowledge, that is, your ability to use pencil and paper methods, while at the same time developing your pedagogical understanding of what you will need to teach children.

The effective development of pencil and paper arithmetic

The government's priorities, identified in the introduction, bring together the notions of procedural fluency in arithmetic and conceptual understanding. The priorities also acknowledge the role of individual schools in making key decisions about the teaching of arithmetic regarding what actually constitutes 'efficient written methods' and also in terms of a timeline for children's progression. This section, and indeed the whole of this book, provides individual teachers as well as curriculum managers with some guiding principles to help them to make informed decisions about these matters.

Using resources including jottings and mental models

In this chapter you will see how jottings are a tool to explain and model mental calculation strategies to children. These jottings are the first stages of pencil and paper arithmetic, demonstrated in the first case study later in this chapter. As was the case with the development of mental arithmetic, you should continue to use a range of models and images to support the teaching of pencil and paper strategies. Number lines, 100 squares, partitioning cards and arrays are just a few examples of the sorts of things you could use to contribute to the development of children's *understanding of the underpinning mathematics,* mentioned in the government's priorities above.

Ensuring progression in the development of children's arithmetical skills

Although the government has stated that *children need to be moved on rapidly to use appropriate efficient written methods* (DfE, 2012a), don't be tempted to rush children too quickly towards using the traditional pencil and paper methods discussed in Chapter 5. It is better for a child to be using the grid method for multiplication and getting correct answers than to be using the traditional method and getting things wrong. The government has not indicated a specific age or year group by which all children should be using efficient written methods and so this is a matter for schools to decide when reviewing mathematics policy documents.

Even when the focus starts to shift towards using pencil and paper methods, continue to encourage children to always use mental arithmetic as a first resort because this mental fluency underpins the development of written methods. The government correctly states that children's arithmetical fluency is also underpinned by understanding concepts such as place value, so you should continue to devote time to this, using bigger numbers and different types of numbers such as decimals. Also continue to spend time developing an understanding of the relationships between operations and the recall of number facts because, again, these underpin arithmetical fluency.

Whose algorithm is it?

Try to give children the freedom to make decisions for themselves, rather than suggesting that there is always a 'correct' or 'best' way of doing it. This freedom could be in selecting the size of the chunks when using the chunking method for division, or the order in which the answers in the cells are added when using grid multiplication, or the choice between starting with the hundreds or the ones when using partitioning-based methods. Teachers often underestimate children's capacity to make decisions and so, with the best intentions, try to eliminate all of the 'nasty bits' when presenting problems to be tackled. If we want children to *solve problems and reason mathematically* (DfE, 2012a) then they must be provided with opportunities to make decisions for themselves.

In terms of ownership and decision making, children will also come up with their own interesting and perfectly valid variations on the methods discussed in the rest of this chapter, so be prepared to let children share, explain and discuss these. This will help to develop the conceptual understanding that the government has identified as a priority.

Engaging parents in developing pencil and paper arithmetic

If you are a younger trainee teacher, you may be confident in using the strategies suggested in this chapter because you were taught in a similar way at school yourself. However, be aware of the fact that some parents may not be familiar with these informal written approaches and so might introduce their children to the traditional methods at an earlier stage than you would wish. Try to make parents aware of the alternatives to the traditional methods through workshops, newsletters, etc. It is important that you present the methods discussed in this chapter to parents and children as being perfectly valid pencil and paper approaches which can be used to solve problems. They should not be viewed as being inferior to the traditional methods or as not being 'the proper way of doing it'.

Using and applying pencil and paper arithmetic

Finally, although the remainder of this chapter focuses on lines of progression with a view to developing your own subject knowledge and equipping you to teach particular techniques, it is vitally important that you provide children with opportunities to use and apply these. This will contribute to the government's aim to *equip them* [children] *for solving unfamiliar problems* (DfE, 2012a).

The first stages of pencil and paper arithmetic

Case Study: Jottings to support multiplication

Bronwyn is teaching mathematics to her mixed ability Year 4 class. They are focusing on the mental multiplication of three-digit numbers by a single digit, starting with multiplication by 2. They are confident in their partitioning of three-digit numbers and so this is the basis of the method they are using to calculate 238×2, as indicated by the dialogue below.

Bronwyn: So we've partitioned it into 200, 30 and 8. Who's going to double the 200 for me?

Asif: 400.

Bronwyn: Good boy – you remember that. Who's going to double the 30?

Victoria: 60.

$\rightarrow$

Bronwyn: Good girl – you can remember that for me. And finally, who's going to double the 8?

Lucy: 16.

Bronwyn: Good. So we've got ... (points at each child)

Asif: 400.

Victoria: 60.

Lucy: 16.

Bronwyn: So what have we got altogether?

Although some children are capable of adding those three numbers together, the majority are finding it difficult because there is nothing written on the board, apart from the original question (238 × 2). Bronwyn therefore provides a visual clue by sticking the three partitioning cards she has been using (200, 30 and 8) on the board. She then asks the three children to call out their parts of the answer (400, 60 and 16) and writes these numbers underneath the corresponding partitioning card. Seeing these three answers, as opposed to having to hold them in their heads, makes the calculation more accessible to the children.

Bronwyn then asks a child to add 400 and 60. She writes the answer (460) underneath and between the two original numbers. Finally, she asks another child to add 460 and 16 and writes down the answer. All of what was written down is shown below.

$$238 \times 2$$

$$\boxed{2\,0\,0} \quad \boxed{3\,0} \quad \boxed{8}$$

$$400 \qquad 60 \qquad 16$$

$$460 + 16 = 476$$

This case study demonstrates the beginnings of pencil and paper arithmetic. Essentially, what is written down are jottings to support a mental calculation, produced because the children doing the calculation are not able to hold all of the intermediate answers in their heads. These early jottings do not have to follow a prescribed format but, as we shall see throughout this chapter, they form the basis of the informal pencil and paper approaches that we should introduce to children during Key Stage 2.

Pencil and paper strategies for addition and subtraction

Activity

Work out the answer to each of the questions below. You can use any method you wish, but you must not use a calculator. If your preferred method is to work out the answer mentally with no written working out, then simply do that, although you might like to think about a written method you are familiar with and jot that down as well.

1. 47 + 36
2. 63 − 28
3. 329 + 253
4. 516 − 434
5. 1025 − 336
6. 5004 − 1947

Keep your answers and any working out you have produced because you can compare your methods with those presented on the following pages. However, before moving on it would be interesting to review how you tackled questions 1 and 2. Did you use any pencil and paper working out or did you do them mentally as your preferred method? If you chose to use pencil and paper, please note that these two questions are of a similar level of difficulty to those you were answering mentally in Chapter 3. Shame on you!

Progression in the development of pencil and paper strategies for addition

Using the empty number line for addition

An empty number line (ENL) is a useful image to use with children to support their mental approaches for addition and to enable increasingly larger numbers to be dealt with. The diagram below shows how an empty number line can be used to work out 47 + 36.

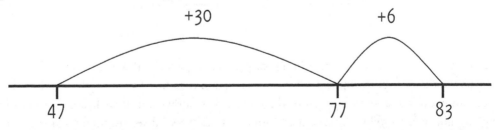

The second number, 36, is partitioned into 30 and 6 and then these two parts are added to 47, by first adding 30 (47 + 30 = 77) and then adding 6 (77 + 6 = 83).

A similar approach could be adopted for 329 + 253, producing the following stages in the calculation:

329 + 200 = 529
529 + 50 = 579
579 + 3 = 582

Research Focus: The empty number line in Dutch schools

Beishuizen (2010) provides a summary of the research that he and his colleagues carried out in the Netherlands during the 1990s as part of the RME (Realistic Mathematics Education) initiative. He starts by providing a simple classification of the ways that children mentally add numbers: the '1010' ('separate tens') approach in which the partitioned 10s and the 1s are added separately, and the 'N10' ('sequence tens') approach in which the first number remains intact and the second number is partitioned into 10s and 1s and added in stages. Research revealed that the more able children favoured the N10 approach and weaker children the 1010 approach, but only a minority of children used both possibilities in a flexible way. The ENL was therefore introduced to encourage flexibility in children's calculating approaches. In addition to the benefit of this enhanced flexibility, Beishuizen provides other arguments for introducing the ENL and also presents evidence indicating that children did indeed adopt more flexible approaches and that weaker pupils improved their levels of performance. With regard to the impact that the research has had in the Netherlands, Beishuizen states that many of the textbooks that are used in Dutch primary schools have been revised and *the ENL model is extended throughout the 3rd grade (Year 4) for number problems up to 1000, followed by the delayed introduction of vertical algorithms until 4th grade (Year 5)* (page 184).

The research by Beishuizen and his colleagues highlights the role of the ENL as a valuable tool to support mental addition strategies and so for many children this should represent their first encounter with pencil and paper methods. However, by the time they are dealing with the addition of three-digit numbers it is likely that they will be utilising alternative approaches like those presented below, based on the partitioning of both numbers.

A key point to be aware of is that the transition from using the ENL to using the partitioning approaches below is not a seamless line of progression. The use of the ENL, based on the 'N10' approach, involves the partitioning of only the second (usually the smaller) number, whereas expanded written methods, based on the '1010' approach, involve the partitioning of both numbers. As Thompson (2010) states *there is actually no logical progression from ENL use to expanded written methods, as they are based on conceptually different procedures.* He also states that *If both numbers are partitioned, you cannot make use of an empty number line (try it!)* (page 189).

Expanded horizontal approaches based on partitioning

Once children are confident in their ability to partition two- and then three-digit numbers, they can utilise this in the expanded horizontal approach for addition presented below.

$$47 + 36 \quad = \quad 40 + 7 + 30 + 6$$
$$= \quad 70 + 13$$
$$= \quad 83$$

Precisely what the children write down by way of working out or explanation is very flexible and will depend upon things such as personal choice, level of confidence, the numbers involved and direction from the teacher. This second example shows less working than the first.

$$329 + 253 = \quad 500 + 70 + 12$$
$$= \quad 582$$

Expanded vertical approaches based on partitioning

The next stage in the progression is to move towards a vertical layout rather than a horizontal one, although the guiding force behind making this shift is the desire for children to eventually be using the traditional compact vertical method discussed in Chapter 5. If the traditional method is not seen as an ultimate goal, then the expanded horizontal and vertical methods can both be viewed as equally valid alternatives, as opposed to being stages through which children must progress. Here are the vertical equivalents to the horizontal representations shown above.

$$
\begin{array}{r}
47 \\
+ \ 36 \\
\hline
70 \\
+ \ 13 \\
\hline
83
\end{array}
\quad
\begin{array}{l}
\text{Say '40 plus 30 equals 70'.} \\
\text{Say '7 plus 6 equals 13'.}
\end{array}
$$

$$
\begin{array}{r}
329 \\
+ \ 253 \\
\hline
500 \\
70 \\
+ \ 12 \\
\hline
582
\end{array}
\quad
\begin{array}{l}
\text{Say '300 plus 200 equals 500'.} \\
\text{Say '20 plus 50 equals 70'.} \\
\text{Say '9 plus 3 equals 12'.}
\end{array}
$$

In all of the expanded approaches presented above, horizontal and vertical, a 'left to right' approach is adopted, that is, the hundreds are added first, followed by the tens, followed by the ones. Research has shown that given the choice, this is the way that most children calculate their answers (Thompson 2010), although in terms of the final answer a 'right to left' approach would be equally valid. However, many teachers, who are intent on making a link with the compact traditional method, insist that children 'start with the ones', which often goes against the children's natural instincts. The simple fact is that the order in which the partitioned numbers are added makes no difference to the answer and so it is important that this is discussed with the children.

Progression in the development of pencil and paper strategies for subtraction

Using the empty number line for subtraction

As with addition, the ENL offers an effective tool to support children's mental subtraction strategies, providing both a valuable visual image as well as a means to jot down intermediate parts of the calculation. The ENL can be utilised in three subtly different ways, depending on the way that the notion of subtraction is being viewed by the child or presented by the teacher.

1. Subtraction as 'taking away'

Children's first encounters with subtraction involve 'taking away', that is, the physical removal of objects. So for $63 - 28$ we would start with 63 objects and physically take away 28 to leave 35. In the context of an ENL we would start at 63 and count back 28 in two steps to see where we land, as illustrated below.

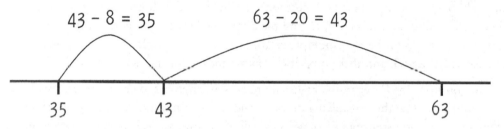

This example involves counting back 20, followed by counting back 8, although there is no reason why this cannot be done in the reverse order, that is, $63 - 8 = 55$ and $55 - 20 = 35$.

2. Subtraction as 'difference' – counting back

Once children understand subtraction as being the difference between the two numbers, the ENL can be utilised in a slightly different way. The answer to $63 - 28$ is the gap between the numbers and this is found by counting back from 63 to 28, as illustrated below.

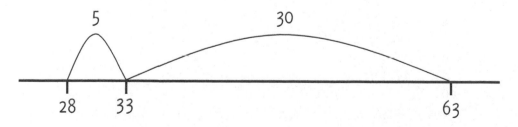

This example shows that the child has counted back from 63 to 33 (a gap of 30), and then counted back from 33 to 28 (a gap of 5), so the overall difference is 35. There is no reason why it has to be done using these two particular steps. For example, another child might choose to utilise multiples of 10 and so count back from 63 to 60 (3), then from 60 to 30 (30) and finally from 30 to 28 (2), again producing an overall difference of 35.

3. Subtraction as 'difference' – counting up

Most people find it easier to count forwards than backwards, and so as soon as children understand subtraction as difference, and also appreciate that you can find the difference by counting in either direction, the ENL can be utilised in a third way, as illustrated below.

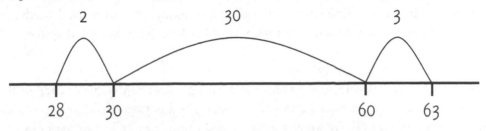

As with the counting back approach, the number and size of the steps is very much a personal choice, although it is important to discuss with the children the choices they make, particularly if they are not efficient ones. Here, to find the difference between 63 and 28, the child has counted on from 28 to the next multiple of 10, then to the multiple of 10 that comes immediately before 63, and then to 63 itself, noting the size of the step each time.

Counting on from the lower to the higher number is an approach that can be used with any subtraction (including those involving decimals and negative numbers), although as children's toolbox of subtraction strategies expands, they will soon come to realise that counting on is at its most efficient when the two numbers are relatively close to one another.

Complementary addition without the number line

Actually drawing a number line is a cumbersome requirement, particularly if the child fully understands the concepts involved and so therefore does not need the visual prop. An alternative is to utilise the counting on approach but without actually drawing the number line, as illustrated below for two of the questions you attempted earlier.

$63 - 28$ =

    28
                (+ 2)
    30
                (+ 30)
    60
                (+ 3)
    63
        (Total 35)

$516 - 434 =$

434

(+ 6)

440

(+ 60)

500

(+ 16)

516

(Total 82)

As with the number line, the choice of steps is a personal one and so, for example, a more confident child may answer the second question using only two steps: from 434 to 500 (66) and from 500 to 516 (16).

An interesting observation, which you might like to share with children, is that if you rotate each of the workings out shown above through 90 degrees anticlockwise, they show a remarkable resemblance to the number line approach, but without the lines being visible.

Subtraction using equivalence

If children understand subtraction as difference, then they should also appreciate that the difference will remain the same if both numbers are increased or decreased by a fixed amount. This generates an equivalent calculation, which will yield the same answer as the original. This is illustrated in the three examples below, again using questions that you tackled earlier.

$63 - 28$ (+ 2)

$65 - 30$

$65 - 30 = 35$

$516 - 434$ (+ 6)

$522 - 440$ (+ 60)

$582 - 500$

$582 - 500 = 82$

$1025 - 336$ (− 25)

$1000 - 311$ (− 11)

$989 - 300$

$989 - 300 = 689$

If you would like to find out more about how children use this approach, which is referred to as 'the same difference' method, see Sugarman (2007).

Vertical subtraction using negative numbers

When using the traditional vertical method to work out $63 - 28$ (see Chapter 5), the commentary provided by the person doing the calculation typically starts with 'three take away eight – you can't do it so ...'. Well actually you can do it, because 3 subtract 8 is negative 5. If children are confident in their ability to understand and manipulate negative numbers, then the following expanded variation on the traditional column method could be used.

$63 - 28 =$

$$
\begin{array}{r}
63 \\
- \ 28 \\
\hline
40 \\
- \ 5 \\
\hline
35 \\
\hline
\end{array}
$$

Say '60 subtract 20 equals 40'.
Say '3 subtract 8 equals negative 5'.
Combine 40 and -5 to give the answer 35.

$1025 - 336 =$

$$
\begin{array}{r}
1025 \\
- \ 336 \\
\hline
700 \\
-10 \\
-1 \\
\hline
689 \\
\hline
\end{array}
$$

Say '1000 subtract 300 equals 700'.
Say '20 subtract 30 equals negative 10'.
Say '5 subtract 6 equals negative 1'.
Combine 700, -10 and -1 to give the answer 689.

Case Study: Children's written methods for subtraction

Derek is a Year 6 teacher and as part of his children's preparation for National Tests in the summer term, he gives them a mathematics paper from a previous year. One of the questions asks the children to calculate $1025 - 336$ without a calculator. Afterwards, he asks four of the children to explain the methods they used. Here are their explanations.

Helen: I subtracted 336 from 1025 and got the answer 689. I did this three times to check my answer. (See the first illustration opposite.)

Tom: I did it mentally. Start with 336, add 4, then add 60, that's 64 altogether. Add 600, you get to a 1000, so that's 664. Now add the extra 25, so that's 689.

Nicky: From 336 I went to 340, which gives me the 4. Then to 400 which is 60. Then you've got the 25 from the 1025 – put that there. Then you add those three together which gives you 89. Then from 400 to 1000 is 600. You add the 600 to the 89 and that gives you 689. (See the second illustration opposite.)

Jack: Calculate 1025 take away 336. I did it in my head. I did 1000 take 300, which is 700. Then I took away 36 which is 664. And then I added the 25 to make 689.

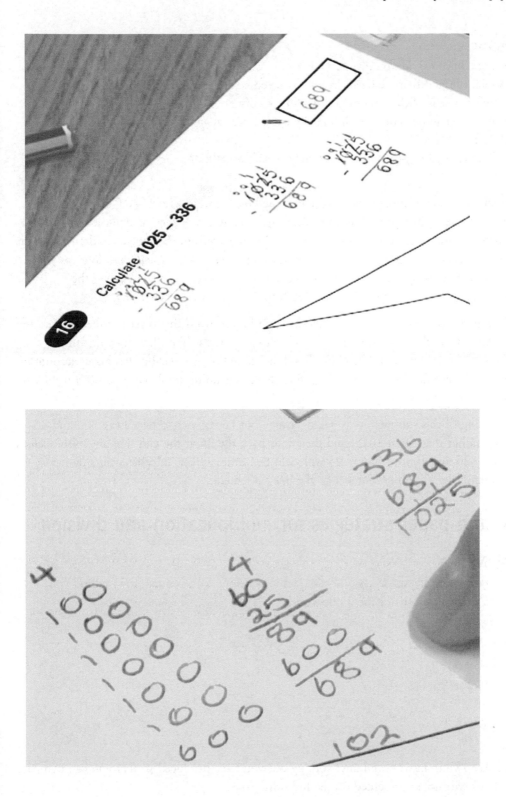

> ## Activity
> What advice would you give to Helen?
> Which method that we have already discussed is Tom using?
> In what way is Nicky's method different to Tom's?
> What other important work has Nicky carried out, apart from what she has spoken about?
> What are the key principles that underpin Jack's method?

Helen has used the traditional pencil and paper method for subtraction (see Chapter 5) but by simply repeating the same procedure three times it is possible that she has replicated an error. Rather than repeating the same method as a checking mechanism, encourage children to use an alternative, for example based on the inverse operation. This is what Nicky has done, as you can see from her working out at the right-hand side of the sheet. As well as doing the subtraction, she has also added her answer (689) to 336, as a way of checking.

Tom is using complementary addition, that is, counting on from the lower number to the higher number to find the difference between the two. Whereas Tom has done this in sequential steps from 336 to 1025, Nicky has done something similar but has taken account of all of the small steps first (4, 60 and 25), before finally including the large step (600) from 400 to 1000.

Jack is thinking of this subtraction as 'taking away', but he chooses to take away 300 and 36 from 1000, rather than from 1025, and then adds back the 25 at the end. He obviously realises that $1025 - 336$ and $1000 - 336 + 25$ will yield the same answer, in other words he has created an equivalent number sentence to the one presented.

Pencil and paper strategies for multiplication and division

> ## Activity
> Work out the answer to each of the questions below. You can use any method you wish, but you must not use a calculator.
>
> 1. 78×6
> 2. $536 \div 8$
> 3. 459×7
> 4. $972 \div 23$
> 5. $125 \div 52$
> 6. $274 \div 62$

As before, keep your answers and any working out you have produced so that you can compare your methods with those presented on the following pages.

Progression in the development of pencil and paper strategies for multiplication

Multiplication as repeated addition

Even when children are still at the stage of using mental methods, as opposed to pencil and paper, they should understand that multiplication can be thought of as repeated addition. So when calculating 78×6 it might be recorded as

$$78 + 78 + 78 + 78 + 78 + 78 = \qquad \text{or as} \qquad \begin{array}{r} 78 \\ 78 \\ 78 \\ 78 \\ 78 \\ + 78 \\ \hline \end{array}$$

although the crucial issue to consider is how the child actually adds these six numbers. If it is repeated addition that is being employed, then the working out is likely to look something like this:

$$\begin{array}{r} 78 \\ + 78 \\ \hline 156 \end{array} \qquad \begin{array}{r} 156 \\ + 78 \\ \hline 234 \end{array} \qquad \begin{array}{r} 234 \\ + 78 \\ \hline 312 \end{array} \qquad \begin{array}{r} 312 \\ + 78 \\ \hline 390 \end{array} \qquad \begin{array}{r} 390 \\ + 78 \\ \hline 468 \end{array}$$

This is a manageable approach as long as there are not too many numbers to be added, but a point is reached where it is more likely that the child will use more than single amounts of the number being multiplied, as demonstrated in the next section.

Repeated doubling

Doubling is a concept that children are introduced to at quite an early age, initially as repeated addition using the notion of 'addition doubles'. Doubling is therefore something that most children are comfortable with. The example below shows the answers when 78 is doubled repeatedly.

$$1 \times 78 = 78$$
$$2 \times 78 = 156$$
$$4 \times 78 = 312$$

So 6×78 can be worked out by adding the second and third answers on the list above:

$$156 + 312 = 468$$

A similar procedure could be used to work out 459×7, as illustrated below.

$$1 \times 459 = \quad 459$$
$$2 \times 459 = \quad 918$$
$$4 \times 459 = 1836$$
$$8 \times 459 = 3672$$

459×7 can be worked out by subtracting 459 from the final answer above:

$$3672 - 459 = 3213$$

An alternative would be to add the first three answers on the list.

Repeated doubling can be used in this way to multiply any numbers; indeed this approach lies at the heart of Egyptian multiplication which is discussed in Chapter 5. However, as the numbers involved become larger, it is usually more efficient to consider alternative approaches based on partitioning, as presented below.

Expanded horizontal approaches based on partitioning

This approach is a 'tidied up' version of the jottings used by the teacher (Bronwyn) in the case study earlier in this chapter. There are also similarities with the expanded horizontal method for addition discussed earlier. Here are two worked examples.

$$
\begin{aligned}
6 \times 78 \quad &= \quad 6 \times 70 + 6 \times 8 \\
&= \quad 420 + 48 \\
&= \quad 468
\end{aligned}
$$

$$
\begin{aligned}
7 \times 459 \quad &= \quad 7 \times 400 + 7 \times 50 + 7 \times 9 \\
&= \quad 2800 + 350 + 63 \\
&= \quad 3213
\end{aligned}
$$

As before, the extent to which children show all of the working out above will depend on personal choice, level of confidence and guidance from the teacher.

Expanded vertical approaches based on partitioning

As with addition, the next stage is to move to a vertical expanded layout, particularly if we want the children to ultimately be familiar with the traditional compact vertical method discussed in Chapter 5.

```
        70
  ×      6
       420        Say '6 multiplied by 70 equals 420'.
  +     48        Say '6 multiplied by 8 equals 48'.
       468
```

$$
\begin{array}{r}
459 \\
\times \quad 7 \\
\hline
2800 \\
350 \\
+ \quad 63 \\
\hline
3213 \\
\end{array}
$$

Say '7 multiplied by 400 equals 2800'.
Say '7 multiplied by 50 equals 350'.
Say '7 multiplied by 9 equals 63'.

The expanded approaches based on partitioning work well when multiplying by a single digit, but for multiplication by two or more digits the setting out of all the calculations can be cumbersome and could lead to some being missed out. An alternative approach, still based on partitioning, is to use the grid method, as explained below.

The 'grid' method

This method can be utilised for the multiplication of any numbers, although it is particularly valuable when multiplying by two or more digits, because its layout provides an effective way of keeping tabs on all of the calculations that contribute to the final answer. Essentially the numbers being multiplied are each partitioned to produce a multiplication grid. The answers for each cell of the grid are calculated and then all of these are added together. Here are three worked examples, using the multiplications you attempted earlier.

78 × 6

Partition 78 and produce a grid.

6	70
420	8
48	468

Calculate answers and add these together.

×	6
70	
8	

×

459 × 7

Partition 459 and produce a grid.

×	7
400	
50	
9	

Calculate answers and add these together.

×	7
400	2800
50	350
9	63

3213

In these first two examples the link between this method and the expanded vertical method should be obvious, with the same intermediate answers being produced for both methods. The third example below illustrates how effective the grid method is when multiplying by more than a single digit.

125 × 52

Partition 125 and 52 to produce a grid.

×	50	2
100		
20		
5		

Calculate answers and add these together.

×	50	2
100	5000	200
20	1000	40
5	250	10

6500

A key consideration is the way that children add the answers in the cells. In the first two examples there are only two or three numbers and so it is fairly straightforward to simply work down the column adding the answers, but not necessarily in the order that they appear. For example, in the grid for 459×7 a child might choose to add 350 and 63 first, before adding this to 2800.

In the final example it would be tempting to insist that children calculate the column totals and then add these together, but this often makes the mental additions more complex than they would otherwise be. Faced with adding the six answers in the grid above a child might prefer to first add 5000 and 1000, and record the answer 6000. The next calculation might be to add 250, 40 and 10, to give 300, then add this to the remaining 200, to give 500, which is recorded. Finally, the recorded numbers (6000 and 500) are added. Children should be encouraged to look for answers that go together easily to make the additions easier, and indeed many children will do this without being prompted. You might ask children to tick each cell once its number has been included, so that none are missed out or counted twice.

An important point that is worth emphasising here is the crucial importance of mental skills. Without the ability to mentally multiply the numbers shown above and to mentally add the answers, children cannot use this method. The grid method therefore contributes to the overall aim of affording mental arithmetic high status in mathematics.

Progression in the development of pencil and paper strategies for division

Division as repeated subtraction

By the time children are tackling division problems involving paper and pencil approaches they should have a good understanding of what division actually is and how it relates to the other arithmetical operations. So when faced with a number sentence such as $31 \div 6$ a child should understand that this can be thought of as 'How many lots of 6 can I get from 31?' and so possibly use repeated subtraction to find the answer. The same approach could be used to tackle one of the divisions you attempted earlier, as illustrated below.

$274 \div 62$

```
   274          212          150           88
 -  62        -  62        -  62         -  62
  ────         ────         ────          ────
   212          150           88           26
```

$274 \div 62 = 4$ remainder 26

Division as repeated addition

Finding how many lots of 62 are in 274 could also be thought of in terms of repeated addition, as shown below.

$274 \div 62$

```
    62          124          186          248           274
 +  62        +  62        +  62        |  62         - 248
  ────         ────         ────         ────          ────
   124          186          248          310            26
```

$274 \div 62 = 4$ remainder 26

The repeated addition and repeated subtraction processes are manageable if the number of required calculations is relatively low. However, with a division such as $536 \div 8$ (which you attempted earlier) the child would have to carry out 67 additions or subtractions. Instead of using single amounts of 8 it would make sense to add or subtract bigger 'bundles' or 'chunks' of 8. This approach is often referred to as the 'chunking' method and is explained in the following sections.

Chunking using multiplication and subtraction

This method involves subtracting larger 'chunks' of the divisor from the dividend as an alternative to using single amounts. Here is a worked example for $536 \div 8$, which is one of the divisions you attempted earlier.

```
        67
    8 )536
     − 400          (50 × 8)
       136
     −  80          (10 × 8)
        56
     −  56          (7 × 8)
         0
```

536 ÷ 8 = 67 with no remainder

By subtracting 50 lots of 8, then 10 lots, and finally 7 lots, the answer of 67, with no remainder, is obtained. The size of the 'chunks' is very much a personal choice and so an able child might immediately spot that 50 lots of 8 can be subtracted (perhaps because she knows that $100 \times 8 = 800$, so 50×8 is half of this), as presented above. Another able child, who is quickly able to calculate $60 \times 8 = 480$ might make use of this as the first chunk. A less confident child might rely on repeatedly subtracting 10 lots, as demonstrated below for 972 ÷ 23.

```
         42
    23 )972
     − 230          (10 × 23)
       742
     − 230          (10 × 23)
       512
     − 230          (10 × 23)
       282
     − 230          (10 × 23)
        52
     −  46          (2 × 23)
         6
```

972 ÷ 23 = 42 remainder 6

The chunking method therefore offers a built-in differentiation mechanism, whereby children will use chunks of a size that they can comfortably deal with. However, in the case of a less able child who relies on subtracting numerous small chunks, the danger is that each calculation offers an opportunity to make a careless error.

Chunking using multiplication and addition

This is a variation on the previous approach and is illustrated below, again using 972 ÷ 23, but with different sized chunks to those used previously.

$$
\begin{array}{ll}
\quad 460 & (20 \times 23) \\
+\ \underline{460} & (20 \times 23) \\
\quad 920 & \\
+\ \underline{\ 46} & (2 \times 23) \\
\quad 966 &
\end{array}
$$

$972 - 966 = 6$ (remainder). So $972 \div 23 = 42$ remainder 6

Research Focus: Children's written methods for division

Anghileri *et al.* (2002) investigated the written methods for division used by Year 5 children in England and the Netherlands. The English children tended to use the traditional method with limited success whereas the Dutch children used chunking approaches and scored well. The authors conclude that:

the Dutch approach, which develops and standardises the informal strategy of repeated subtraction, leads to a procedure that pupils are confident to use and that they use effectively. Because this procedure can be used at different levels of efficiency an element of choice is retained so the pupils continue to have some ownership of the thinking within the structured approach.

(Anghileri et al., 2002, page 167)

and that

Learning is most effective where written methods build upon pupils' intuitive understanding in a progressive way. Informal solution methods may be inefficient, but support in structuring such approaches in a written record appears to lead to better efficiency gains than replacing them with a standard procedure. Application of taught methods can become mechanistic and unthinking where pupils are unclear about the links between a taught procedure and the meanings they can identify. Application of taught methods becomes the first imperative and appears to inhibit more thoughtful approaches that take account of problem structure and the numbers involved.

(Anghileri et al., 2002, page 168)

Learning Outcomes Review

You should now understand that children's first encounters with pencil and paper arithmetic should not be the traditional methods. Instead, the first pencil and paper approaches that are introduced to children should be based on their mental strategies, developing naturally from an inability to manipulate the numbers mentally and hold all the answers in their heads. In order to develop and utilise the methods discussed in this chapter, children must possess good mental skills, must understand place value and must be aware of the relationships between the four operations.

It is also important for you to appreciate the status of the methods discussed in this chapter. They should never be seen as being inferior to the traditional pencil and paper methods discussed in the next chapter. They are perfectly valid and, in most cases, very efficient ways of obtaining correct answers. They may take up more space than the more compact traditional methods, but for many children they provide a more accessible alternative, and at the same time they give the teacher a better insight into children's understanding. If children are comfortable with the non-traditional approaches then care should be taken before moving them out of this comfort zone.

Self-assessment questions
Answer the following questions using any approaches you wish, apart from the traditional compact pencil and paper methods.

1. $714 - 368$
2. $837 + 588$
3. 43×517
4. $1049 \div 37$ (use remainders rather than decimals)

Further Reading

QCA (1999) *Teaching Written Calculations: Guidance for teachers at Key Stages 1 and 2*. Sudbury: QCA Publications.

Thompson, I. (1994) Young children's idiosyncratic written algorithms for addition, *Educational Studies in Mathematics*, 26(4): 323–45.

Thompson, I. (1997) Mental and written algorithms: can the gap be bridged?, in Thompson, I. (ed.) *Teaching and Learning Early Number* (1st edition). Buckingham: Open University Press.

Thompson, I. (2010) Progression in the teaching of multiplication, in Thompson, I. (ed.) *Issues in Teaching Numeracy in Primary Schools*. Maidenhead: Open University Press.

Thompson, I. (2010) Progression in the teaching of division, in Thompson, I. (ed.) *Issues in Teaching Numeracy in Primary Schools*. Maidenhead: Open University Press.

References

Anghileri, J., Beishuizen, M. and Van Putten, K. (2002) From informal strategies to structured procedures: mind the gap! *Educational Studies in Mathematics*, 49: 149–70.

Beishuizen, M. (2010) The empty number line, in Thompson, I. (ed.) *Issues in Teaching Numeracy in Primary Schools*. Maidenhead: Open University Press.

DfE (2012a) *Key priorities for arithmetic*. Presentation to ITT mathematics tutors, TDA/UCET/ NASBTT conference for Primary ITT tutors, Lancaster and London. March, 2012.

DfE (2012b) *National Curriculum for Mathematics: Key Stages 1 and 2 – Draft*. London: DfE Publications.

DfEE (1999) *The National Numeracy Strategy: Framework for Teaching Mathematics*. Sudbury: DfEE Publications.

National Strategies (2011) *Guidance Paper: Calculation*. London: DfE Publications. Available at: http://webarchive.nationalarchives.gov.uk/20110202093118/http://nationalstrategies.standards. dcsf.gov.uk/node/47364?uc=force_uj (accessed June 2012).

Sugarman, I. (2007) The same difference. *Mathematics Teaching*, 202: 16–18.

Thompson, I. (2010) Written calculation: addition and subtraction, in Thompson, I. (ed.) *Issues in Teaching Numeracy in Primary Schools*. Maidenhead: Open University Press.

5. Traditional pencil and paper arithmetic

Learning Outcomes

By the end of this chapter you will:

- be familiar with the traditional pencil and paper arithmetic methods for addition, subtraction, multiplication and division;
- understand why these traditional methods work;
- be aware of the benefits and potential problems associated with the traditional methods;
- have considered some of the common errors and misconceptions made by children when using these methods.

Introduction

Before the traditional pencil and paper methods for addition, subtraction, multiplication and division are presented in detail, it is important to first consider the benefits and potential problems associated with these approaches.

Activity

Think carefully about the traditional pencil and paper methods that you know, for example addition with 'carrying', subtraction with 'borrowing', long multiplication and long division. You might like to make up some questions and try the methods, just as a reminder.

1. What are the benefits offered by these traditional methods?
2. What are the potential difficulties associated with these methods?
3. Make a list of benefits and potential difficulties.

Compare your list with the points that are presented below. When you have studied the whole of this chapter it might be beneficial to revisit these points and reflect further on the implications.

Benefits offered by traditional pencil and paper arithmetic

They are compact and so children will use less paper and fewer exercise books. Traditional methods are therefore good for the environment.

They are reliable. In other words, if you follow the procedures correctly you will always get the correct answer, in the same way that if you follow a baking recipe precisely you will always get a perfect cake.

They can be used with numbers of any size, either whole numbers or decimals. It is also worth noting that conceptually it is no more difficult to add two two-digit numbers, than two ten-digit numbers because the procedure remains the same, although the more digits there are, the greater the potential to make a mistake.

They are not dependent upon any mathematical understanding and so, in theory, anyone can be trained to use them in a relatively short space of time, which means that it is possible to achieve positive outcomes (that is, correct answers) shortly after introducing a procedure. Those who are driven by the pressures of tests and examinations see this as a particular benefit.

They are widely known and so teachers from a range of backgrounds and locations will be familiar with the procedures, although, as we shall see later, there are variations in the way that they are executed.

They are easy for teachers to mark and there is nothing more pleasing for children and their parents than to see a neat page of 'sums' with lots of ticks.

Potential difficulties associated with traditional pencil and paper arithmetic

In terms of progression they do not build on children's previous experiences of the mental and informal pencil and paper approaches discussed in Chapters 3 and 4. Therefore, for many children they are presented almost from nowhere as a new method to use.

They require children to remember a set of rules rather than understand the arithmetical process that is being carried out, resulting in a loss of ownership in the learning process. We should not automatically assume that all children just want to know 'how to do it' without any understanding of 'how' and 'why'.

They encourage children to focus on the individual digits rather than the numbers in their entirety and so children lose sight of what the digits actually represent as hundreds, tens, ones, etc. It is therefore possible for a child to have no understanding at all of two- and three-digit numbers, but at the same time get correct answers to two- and three-digit additions and subtractions.

Because they rely solely on the manipulation of digits, they cannot be related to the real world or utilise any effective models or images to aid children's understanding. Base 10 blocks have been used by teachers in the past to support the teaching of traditional arithmetic, but, as we shall see in a research focus later in this chapter, they are not as effective as some might think.

Despite supposedly being 'standard' methods, there are many variations and inconsistencies which only serve to confuse children. Examples of this include the fact that there are two traditional methods for subtraction, and also the different ways of recording the 'carries' when doing additions and multiplications. We will look at this in more detail later in the chapter.

They do not always offer the most efficient approach. Ask two children to calculate 199 + 105, one using traditional column addition and the other using mental methods, and see who gets the answer first. You could carry out a similar speed test using calculations such as $203 - 198$ or 199×3.

They can lead to the blind acceptance of results, possibly because children may have no understanding of what the numbers themselves actually represent in terms of size or quantity, and possibly because they are simply following a mechanical process to produce an answer, but without any consideration as to whether it looks reasonable.

Because they are perceived as being the 'proper way of doing it', once introduced they result in children abandoning the mental and informal pencil and paper methods that they were very happy to use previously, and often with much success.

Despite many years of repeated practice, some children are not able to master the techniques.

They tend not to be used by many adults and children, apart from in mathematics lessons.

So where does that leave the teacher?

Despite the strong arguments presented in Chapters 3 and 4 for a greater emphasis on mental arithmetic and informal pencil and paper methods, and the potential difficulties with traditional pencil and paper arithmetic identified above, it is a fact that the traditional methods are here to stay. As discussed at the start of Chapter 4, the Department for Education has stated that

- *Children must be fluent in applying quick, efficient written methods of calculation.*

(DfE, 2012a)

More recently the government has published draft programmes of study for mathematics (DfE, 2012b) which state that children should be taught 'reliable' and 'efficient' written methods, although the expression 'formal written methods' does appear with much greater frequency. However, one could argue that 'quick', 'reliable' and 'efficient' methods are not necessarily the same as the traditional compact methods (or 'formal' methods as they are called in the draft programmes of study) that will be discussed in this chapter. Many of the approaches presented in Chapter 4 can be quick, reliable and efficient. Nevertheless, it is likely that most schools will choose to incorporate the teaching of traditional written methods into their mathematics policies and so the following guiding principles are offered.

- The traditional methods should be seen as the final stage in children's progression through a range of approaches to pencil and paper arithmetic. The earlier stages in this progression have already been considered in Chapter 4.

- Some children might not reach this final stage of the progression by the time they leave primary school. You might need to ask yourself questions such as: 'Would I prefer a child to use the grid method for multiplication and get correct answers, or keep failing with the traditional method for long multiplication?' After all, a method is not 'efficient' if you keep getting the answers wrong.

- When traditional pencil and paper arithmetic is introduced this does not mean that mental arithmetic and informal pencil and paper methods should be abandoned. The approaches discussed in Chapters 3 and 4 should continue to be reinforced and developed throughout a child's education.

- Traditional pencil and paper approaches should never be presented as the 'proper', 'correct' or 'best' way of doing a calculation. They may offer an efficient, compact solution in some circumstances, but on other occasions there will be better alternatives, such as mental methods.

- When teaching traditional pencil and paper methods, try to ensure that children can see how these relate to the informal methods they already know. For example, discuss the links between the intermediate answers generated when using the grid method of multiplication and those obtained when using the traditional method. This will help children to understand why the traditional methods work, in the same way that you will understand when you have studied the rest of this chapter.

- When teaching the traditional methods, consistency can help to avoid some of the common problems that children encounter. Schools should therefore have a policy which states, for example, where the 'carries' are recorded in an addition or multiplication. As a trainee or new teacher in a school, it is important to establish what the recognised conventions are and to adhere to these.

- If children are getting answers wrong, it is absolutely vital to diagnose the specific misconception or careless error so that targeted support can be provided to correct it. In some cases it might be necessary to abandon the traditional approaches in favour of a previously taught alternative.

Research Focus: *Decomposition and all that rot*

Over 30 years ago Plunkett (1979) wrote what has become a seminal and much cited article which considers the nature of traditional written algorithms and the way that they are used by adults and children. He provides a ten-point summary of the characteristics of traditional algorithms and concludes that they tend not to be used, they are not understood and they are often misused when a more efficient alternative exists. He contrasts these methods with the nature of mental arithmetic, again providing a concise list of key characteristics. He concludes by stating that:

> *a large amount of time is at present wasted on attempts to teach and learn the standard algorithms, and that the most common results are frustration, unhappiness and a deteriorating attitude to mathematics.*

(page 4)
→

> Plunkett's arguments remain relevant today and so it is strongly recommended that you consult this article and reflect upon its implications. If you struggle to find a copy, instead consult O'Sullivan *et al.* (2005) which provides lengthy extracts from the original as well as an analysis of the content.

Traditional methods for addition

The traditional 'carrying' method for addition, set out in columns, is one that nearly all children are taught by the time they leave primary school. Depending on the era when you were at primary school yourself, you may have been taught this method at as young as 5 or 6 years old, although more recently its introduction has tended to be delayed until lower to middle Key Stage 2.

When using the traditional 'carrying' method to calculate 365 + 87 it would be set out like this:

```
    3 6 5
+     8 7
  ———————
```

Activity

Use the traditional 'carrying' method to work out the answer to 365 + 87.

Think carefully about the common errors that children might make when tackling this question. Try to list as many errors as possible.

Here is a step-by-step breakdown of how you could have set out your answer:

Step 1

```
    3 6 5      5 add 7 equals 12.
+     8₁7      'Carry' the 1 in the tens column and write down the 2 ones.
  ———————
        2
```

Step 2

```
    3 6 5      6 add 8 add 1 equals 15 (it is actually 60 add 80 add 10 equals 150).
+   ₁8₁7       'Carry' the 1 in the hundreds column and write down the 5 tens.
  ———————
      5 2
```

Step 3

```
  3 6 5     3 add 1 equals 4 (it is actually 300 add 100 equals 400).
+  ₁8₁7     Write down the 4 hundreds.
  4 5 2
```

Can you see how this traditional method is a compact equivalent of the expanded pencil and paper method that was discussed in Chapter 4? Perhaps use the expanded method to work out the answer and compare this with the more compact traditional approach shown above.

Variations

Common variations on this layout would be to write the 'carries' at the top of each column or underneath the lower horizontal line, as shown below.

```
  3¹ 6¹ 5            3  6  5
+     8  7         +    8  7
  4  5  2           4  5  2
                    1     1
```

All of these variations are perfectly acceptable; the important issue is that any 'carries' are actually recorded and not omitted in subsequent stages of the calculation.

Children's addition errors

Here are some of the more common possible errors. As with all errors made by children, the key role of the teacher is to diagnose specifically what the nature of the error is and then address it in a targeted way, rather than simply re-teaching the method. For each of the examples given below you might like to think about what sort of targeted support you would give the child, so as to remedy the error.

• Left-justifying the numbers.

```
    3 6 5
+   8 7
  _____
```

• Avoiding any carrying by writing two-digit answers between the horizontal lines (5 + 7 = 12 and 6 + 8 = 14).

```
    3 6 5
+    8 7
  3 1 4 1 2
```

• Transposing the two-digit answers in terms of where they are placed (for example 5 + 7 = 12 but carry the 2 and write the 1 between the lines).

```
    3 6 5
+   ₆8 ₂7
  9 1 1
```

- Writing down the correct 'carries' but forgetting to include them when adding up the next column

$$
\begin{array}{r}
3\ 6\ 5 \\
+\ \ {}_1 8_1\ 7 \\
\hline
3\ 4\ 2
\end{array}
$$

Research Focus: 'Column value' and 'quantity value' revisited

Please revisit the research focus in Chapter 3 which highlights the work of Thompson (2009) and Thompson and Bramald (2002) who consider the 'column value' and 'quantity value' aspects of place value. They argue that the traditional definition of place value, which would explain the number 83 as '8 in the tens column' or '8 lots of 10', is an outdated one and is only relevant when teaching the traditional pencil and paper methods. In contrast, 'quantity value', which is utilised by most people when working mentally, considers 83 in terms of '80 and 3'.

Traditional methods for subtraction: by decomposition

The traditional 'borrowing' method discussed here is the one that most children are taught at school. There is another traditional method (by equal addition) which will be looked at shortly.

When using the traditional decomposition ('borrowing') method to calculate $645 - 187$ it would be set out like this:

$$
\begin{array}{r}
6\ 4\ 5 \\
-\ 1\ 8\ 7 \\
\hline
 \\
\hline
\end{array}
$$

Activity
Use the traditional decomposition ('borrowing') method to work out the answer to $645 - 187$.

Here is a step-by-step breakdown of how you could have set out your answer.

Step 1

$$
\begin{array}{r}
6\ {}^3\!\!\!\not4\ {}^1 5 \\
-\ 1\ 8\ 7 \\
\hline
8
\end{array}
$$

Subtract 7 from 5. This cannot be done (without using negative numbers) so borrow 10 from the 4 tens in the adjacent column, to leave 3 tens (cross out the 4 and replace with 3). The 5 ones now becomes 15. Subtract 7 from 15 to leave 8.

Step 2

$^5\cancel{6}$ $^{13}\cancel{4}$ ^{1}5

− 1 8 7

5 8

Subtract 8 from 3 in the tens column. This cannot be done (without using negative numbers) so borrow 100 from the six hundreds in the adjacent column, to leave 5 hundreds (cross out the 6 and replace with 5). The 3 tens now becomes 13 tens. Subtract 8 from 13 to leave 5.

Step 3

$^5\cancel{6}$ $^{13}\cancel{4}$ ^{1}5

− 1 8 7

4 5 8

Finally, in the hundreds column, subtract 1 from 5 to leave 4.

If you have mastered this technique you probably carry out arithmetic like this without even thinking about it. But have you ever thought about precisely what is happening when you borrow?

Activity

Look carefully at the numbers in Step 1 and Step 2 of the calculation above. In what ways has the top number changed? Is the top number still 645 at each step? Explain how you know.

The bottom number remains as 187 throughout the calculation.

The top number is initially written as

6 hundreds (600)   4 tens (40)   5 ones (5)   which is 645.

At the end of Step 1, it is now written as

6 hundreds (600)   3 tens (30)   15 ones (15)   which is still 645.

At the end of Step 2, it is now written as

5 hundreds (500)   13 tens (130)   15 ones (15)   which is still 645.

So throughout the calculation, the top number is always 645, but on two occasions it is 'decomposed' in different ways across the hundreds, tens and ones columns.

'Borrowing' or 'exchanging'?

The expression 'borrowing' has been used to describe the traditional method presented above, because this is widely used by teachers when modelling the procedure for children. However, 'borrowing' implies that something is going to be given back later, but clearly this does not happen. A preferable alternative expression is therefore 'exchanging'. So in the example above, instead of saying 'Borrow 10 from the 4 tens to give 15 in the ones column' say '*Exchange* one of the 4 tens for 10 ones, to give 15 in the ones column'. The expression 'exchange' will be used in all further explanations of the decomposition method in this chapter.

Children's decomposition errors

Here are some of the typical errors that children might make when tackling this question.

- Left-justifying the numbers, although in this case it would not matter, but if you were subtracting a two-digit number from a three-digit number it would.

- Avoiding any exchanging by always taking the smaller digit from the larger, regardless of where the digits are.

$$\begin{array}{r} 6\ 4\ 5 \\ -1\ 8\ 7 \\ \hline 5\ 4\ 2 \end{array}$$

- Recognising that exchanging will have to be done on two occasions, why not exchange 2 from the hundreds column and give one each of these to the tens and the ones?

$$\begin{array}{r} {}^{4}\cancel{6}\ {}^{1}4\ {}^{1}5 \\ -1\ 8\ 7 \\ \hline 3\ 6\ 8 \end{array}$$

Can you see why this is wrong? What has 645 become after this sort of decomposition?

It has now become

4 hundreds (400)   14 tens (140)   15 ones (15)   which is 555.

So 645 has been reduced to 555, therefore producing an answer which is out by 90.

Just in case you found the traditional decomposition method challenging, here is a step-by-step breakdown.

Step 1

$$\begin{array}{r} {}^{4}\!\!\not{5}\quad {}^{1}0\quad 0\quad 4 \\ -\,1\quad 9\quad 4\quad 7 \\ \hline \end{array}$$

Subtract 7 from 4. This cannot be done (without using negative numbers). It's not possible to exchange in the tens (0) or in the hundreds (0), so exchange one of the 5 thousands to leave 4 thousands (cross out the 5 and replace with 4). The 1 thousand is exchanged for 10 hundreds in the hundreds column.

Step 2

$$\begin{array}{r} {}^{4}\!\!\not{5}\quad {}^{9}\!\!\not{\!1}0\quad {}^{1}0\quad 4 \\ -\,1\quad 9\quad 4\quad 7 \\ \hline \end{array}$$

Exchange 1 of the 10 hundreds to leave 9 hundreds (cross out the 10 and replace with 9). The 1 hundred is exchanged for 10 tens in the tens column.

Step 3

$$\begin{array}{r} {}^{4}\!\!\not{5}\quad {}^{9}\!\!\not{\!1}0\quad {}^{9}\!\!\not{\!1}0\quad {}^{1}4 \\ -\,1\quad 9\quad 4\quad 7 \\ \hline \end{array}$$

Exchange 1 of the 10 tens to leave 9 tens (cross out the 10 and replace with 9). The 1 ten is exchanged for 10 ones in the ones column.

Step 4

$$\begin{array}{r} {}^{4}\!\!\not{5}\quad {}^{9}\!\!\not{\!1}0\quad {}^{9}\!\!\not{\!1}0\quad {}^{1}4 \\ -\,1\quad 9\quad 4\quad 7 \\ \hline 3\quad 0\quad 5\quad 7 \end{array}$$

Finally, subtract 7 from 14, subtract 4 from 9, subtract 9 from 9, and subtract 1 from 4.

Having tried this method yourself or by working through the steps above, you will appreciate how unnecessarily complex we sometimes make calculations for children. Given a free choice it is hoped that you opted for a more efficient method to work out the answer, based around counting on from the lower number to the higher. You may have been able to do this entirely as a mental calculation or you may have jotted a few things down, in a similar fashion to the approaches discussed in Chapters 3 and 4.

Sadly, there are possibly some teachers who are insisting that children use the traditional decomposition method for calculations like the one above, when clearly it would be more appropriate to use an efficient alternative. Sometimes the requirement to use decomposition is explicit; on other occasions it is implicit in the way that the calculation is presented vertically in columns, as opposed to a horizontal number sentence. Next time you are in a bookshop, browse through the pages of some of the Key Stage 2 workbooks that are available and see how many examples of this you can find. You won't have to look for too long!

4943 is generated by always taking the smaller digit from the larger, even if the larger number is at the bottom.

1167 is generated by exchanging 3 of the 5 thousands, to leave 2 thousands, and giving one to the hundreds, one to the tens and one to the ones.

Traditional methods for subtraction: by equal addition

Although not as common as the decomposition method discussed above, subtraction by 'equal addition' is a method that has been taught by many teachers in the past, often being described using expressions such as 'borrowing and paying back on the doorstep'. Because you may not be familiar with this method, it will be explained step-by-step, using the same number sentence that was used for the decomposition method earlier (645 − 187).

Step 1

Subtract 7 from 5. This cannot be done (without using negative numbers) so borrow 1 from the tens column in order to change the 5 ones to 15. Also pay back 1 'on the doorstep' by placing a 1 next to the 8. The point to remember is that this is 1 + 8 i.e. 9 tens, not 18 tens.

Step 2

$$6\ ^14\ ^15$$
$$-\ _11\ _18\ 7$$
$$\underline{\qquad\quad 8}$$

Subtract 7 from 15 to leave 8.
Subtract 9 (1 + 8) from 4 in the tens column. This cannot be done (without using negative numbers) so borrow 1 in order to change the 4 ones to 14 and pay back 1 on the doorstep.

Step 3

$$6\ ^14\ ^15$$
$$-\ _11\ _18\ 7$$
$$\underline{4\ 5\ 8}$$

Subtract 9 (1 + 8) from 14 in the tens column to leave 5.
Subtract 2 (1 + 1) from 6 in the hundreds column to leave 4.

As with the decomposition method, it is vitally important that you understand why it works and the possible pitfalls that children might encounter.

Activity

Study this method carefully and consider the following questions.

1. Which aspects of the procedure and the notation might cause confusion?
2. Look carefully at the numbers at Step 1 and Step 2 of the calculation above. In what ways have the two numbers changed? Is the top number still 645 and the bottom number still 187 at each step? Explain how you know.
3. Why does this method work, that is, what is actually happening when you 'borrow and pay back'?

In terms of the language, the notion of 'borrowing and paying back' is an interesting one because it is not obvious where you are actually borrowing from and it is certainly not from the place where you pay back!

The notation is also a possible source of confusion for children. When you 'borrow', you place a 1 in front of the existing digit and this represents 10. So, by way of example, the 5 in Step 1 above becomes 15. When you 'pay back' you place a 1 in front of the existing digit and this represents one more than what is there already. So children have to remember that placing a 1 in front of a digit can have two very different meanings.

Both numbers change at various stages of the calculation.

The top number is initially written as

| 6 hundreds (600) | 4 tens (40) | 5 ones (5) | which is 645. |

At the end of Step 1, it is now written as

| 6 hundreds (600) | 4 tens (40) | 15 ones (15) | which is 655. |

At the end of Step 2, it is now written as

| 6 hundreds (600) | 14 tens (140) | 15 ones (15) | which is 755. |

The bottom number is initially written as

| 1 hundred (100) | 8 tens (80) | 7 ones (7) | which is 187. |

At the end of Step 1, it is now written as

| 1 hundred (100) | 9 tens (90) | 7 ones (7) | which is 197. |

At the end of Step 2, it is now written as

| 2 hundreds (200) | 9 tens (90) | 7 ones (7) | which is 297. |

So the calculations starts as   645 − 187 =

Then at the end of Step 1 becomes   655 − 197 =

Then finally becomes   755 − 297 =

The answer to all three calculations is 458 because at each stage the same amount has been added to both numbers; 10 at Step 1 and 100 at Step 2. Because we are calculating the *difference* between the two numbers, we can increase or decrease both numbers by an equal amount and leave the answer unchanged. You should now understand why this method is called subtraction by equal addition.

Activity

Use the traditional equal addition ('borrowing and paying back on the doorstep') method to work out the answer to $5004 - 1947$.

How easy is it to use this method compared with the decomposition method?

Here is a step-by-step breakdown of the method.

Step 1

$$5 \ 0 \ 0 \ {}^{1}4$$
$$- \ 1 \ 9 \ {}_{1}4 \ 7$$
$$ 7$$

Subtract 7 from 4. This cannot be done (without using negative numbers) so borrow 1 in order to change the 4 ones to 14. Also pay back 1 'on the doorstep' by placing a 1 next to the 4, so that this becomes 5 tens. Subtract 7 from 14 to leave 7.

Step 2

$$5 \ 0 \ {}^{1}0 \ {}^{1}4$$
$$- \ 1{}_{1}9 \ {}_{1}4 \ 7$$
$$ 5 \ 7$$

Subtract 5 from 0. This cannot be done (without using negative numbers) so borrow 1 in order to change the 0 to 10. Also pay back 1 'on the doorstep' by placing a 1 next to the 9, so that this becomes 10 hundreds. Subtract 5 from 10 to leave 5.

Step 3

$$5 \ {}^{1}0 \ {}^{1}0 \ {}^{1}4$$
$$-{}_{1}1 \ {}_{1}9 \ {}_{1}4 \ 7$$
$$ 3 \ 0 \ 5 \ 7$$

Subtract 10 from 0. This cannot be done (without using negative numbers) so borrow 1 in order to change the 0 to 10. Also pay back 1 'on the doorstep' by placing a 1 next to the 1, so that this becomes 2 hundreds. Subtract 10 from 10 to leave 0. Finally subtract 2 from 5 to leave 3.

Once you have mastered the technique, the 'borrowing and paying back' method is probably easier to use than decomposition, particularly when there are zeros in the top number, as in the example above. However, it should be remembered that the 'borrowing and paying back' method tends not to be taught nowadays and so decomposition is recognised as being the accepted compact traditional pencil and paper method for subtraction. Having said that, it should also be remembered that mental and informal pencil and paper methods sometimes offer a more efficient alternative to the traditional approach, as discussed in Chapters 3 and 4.

Research Focus: Using base 10 blocks to model traditional written methods

Dienes' base 10 blocks became popular in the 1960s as a way of developing children's understanding of place value and as a visual aid to assist the modelling of the 'carrying' and 'exchanging' processes associated with the traditional written methods for addition and subtraction. Over the last forty years there has been much discussion about the effectiveness of this sort of equipment. At the same time there has been a gradual reduction in the use of it in favour of alternatives such as number lines and partitioning (HTU) cards. Houssart (2000) interviewed a sample of Key Stage 2 teachers towards the end of the first year of the implementation of the National Numeracy Strategy and found *a lack of enthusiasm for pre-strategy resources, such as base ten blocks* (page 41). She also identifies research evidence that questions *the assumption that children could make the link between physical manipulation of the blocks and the pencil and paper procedures they were said to be related to* (page 37).

Hart (1987) presents the results of research involving 8- and 9-year-old children using base 10 blocks to demonstrate the exchanging process during decomposition. She concludes by questioning the effectiveness of the equipment in developing an understanding of subtraction in the ways we expect it to. Boulton-Lewis (1998) attributes this lack of effectiveness to the huge processing load that it places upon children's cognitive resources. She contends that:

> *Although children can physically manipulate the objects, and allocate the appropriate names, they cannot recognize the structural correspondence between the concrete representation and the mathematical concept it is intended to illustrate.*

> (Boulton-Lewis, 1998, page 222)

Her research also revealed that by Year 3 very few children were choosing to use the apparatus, preferring instead to use mental strategies based on their understanding of place value, with these strategies proving to be more successful than the written alternatives. She concludes by saying that the children's preference not to use the apparatus confirms the heavy processing load that it places upon them, and that the only way that the apparatus can be used effectively is by getting the children to the stage where they are using it automatically.

McNeil and Jarvin (2007) reach similar conclusions to those of Boulton-Lewis, stating that the blocks require dual representation, that is, they are physical objects in their own right, but are also a symbolic representation of a mathematical

$\rightarrow$

procedure. This dual representation, they say, is very demanding in terms of children's cognitive resources. They also believe that teachers' motives for using the apparatus often relate more to making their lessons more fun and varied, than to a genuine belief that it is an effective aid to the development of mathematical concepts and procedures.

Traditional methods for multiplication

The distinction between 'short' and 'long' multiplication is based on the size of the numbers involved. Traditionally, if you are multiplying by a number up to 12 it is short multiplication. Multiplication by a number greater than 12 is considered to be long multiplication. The boundary is tied to beliefs about which multiplication facts children should be able to recall instantly. Historically this has been up to 12×12, stemming from the fact that our previous currency system had twelve pennies in a shilling and because there are 12 inches in a foot. Today, however, there are strong arguments for the upper limit being 10×10 because, for example, you can use your knowledge of these facts to quickly work out others, such as 12×8. Ultimately the decision about how you treat a multiplier is yours, and so you must decide whether you would prefer to mentally multiply by a two-digit number such as 12, or alternatively multiply by 10 and 2 as two distinct stages.

Traditional methods for multiplication: short multiplication

When using the traditional method of short multiplication to calculate 496×8 it would be set out like this:

```
    4 9 6
×       8
  ───────
```

Activity

Use the traditional method you are familiar with, which probably involves 'carrying', to work out the answer to 496×8.

Think carefully about the common errors that children might make when tackling this question. Try to list as many errors as possible.

Here is a step-by-step breakdown of how you could have set out your answer:

Step 1

```
    4 9 6     6 multiplied by 8 equals 48.
×   ₄ 8       'Carry' the 4 in the tens column and write down the 8 ones.
      8
```

Step 2

$\begin{array}{r} 4\ 9\ 6 \\ \times\ \ _7\ _4\ 8 \\ \hline 6\ 8 \end{array}$ 9 multiplied by 8, plus the 4 carried, equals 76 (it is actually 90 multiplied by 8, plus 40 equals 760).

'Carry' the 7 in the hundreds column and write down the 6 tens.

Step 3

$\begin{array}{r} 4\ 9\ 6 \\ \times\ \ _7\ _4\ 8 \\ \hline 3\ 9\ 6\ 8 \end{array}$ 4 multiplied by 8, plus the 7 carried, equals 39 (it is actually 400 multiplied by 8, plus 700 equals 3900).

Write down the 39 hundreds.

Can you see how this traditional method is a compact equivalent of the expanded pencil and paper method that was discussed in Chapter 4? Perhaps you could use the expanded method to work out the answer and compare this with the more compact traditional approach shown above.

Variations

Common variations on this layout would be to write the 'carries' at the top of each column or underneath the lower horizontal line, as shown below.

$\begin{array}{r} 4^7\ 9^4\ 6 \\ \times\ \ \ \ \ \ \ \ 8 \\ \hline 3\ 9\ 6\ 8 \end{array}$ $\begin{array}{r} 4\ \ 9\ \ 6 \\ \times\ \ \ \ \ \ \ \ 8 \\ \hline 3\ 9\ 6\ 8 \\ {\scriptstyle 7\ \ \ 4} \end{array}$

Children's multiplication errors

The common errors that children make are largely related to the 'carries' and are similar to those discussed earlier in this chapter when considering the traditional method for addition. Please refer back to that section to remind yourself of the sorts of errors that are commonly made.

Traditional methods for multiplication: long multiplication

When using the traditional method of long multiplication to calculate 415×26 it would be set out like this:

$\begin{array}{r} 4\ 1\ 5 \\ \times\ \ \ 2\ 6 \\ \hline \end{array}$

Here is a step-by-step breakdown of the traditional method:

Step 1

```
      4  1  5
×       2₃ 6
   2  4  9  0
```

Multiply 415 by 6, using the short multiplication method described
above to give the answer 2490.

Step 2

```
      4  1  5
×    ₁ 2₃ 6
   2  4  9  0
   8  3  0  0
```

Multiply 415 by 20, by first writing down a zero and then multiplying
by 2 using the short multiplication method described above.
The answer, 8300, is written below 2490. Any carries (just '1' in this
example, when you work out $2 \times 5 = 10$) must be squeezed in
somewhere.

Step 3

```
      4  1  5
×    ₁ 2₃ 6
   2  4  9  0
 ₁ 8  3  0  0
 1 0  7  9  0
```

Add 2490 and 8300 using the traditional method for addition described
earlier in this chapter.

Can you see how this traditional method generates the same intermediate answers as the 'grid'
method of multiplication discussed in Chapter 4? In Step 1 above, the calculations are
$5 \times 6 = 30$, $10 \times 6 = 60$ and $400 \times 6 = 2400$. In Step 2 three more multiplications are carried
out. Perhaps use the grid method to work out 415×26 and compare this to the more compact
traditional approach shown above.

Variations on this layout would be to write the 'carries' in alternative locations, as discussed
earlier in this chapter.

Another variation is to multiply by the 2 (i.e. 20) first and then by the 6. Can you see why this
will not affect the answer, as long as other aspects of the method are executed correctly?

Children's multiplication errors

As with the traditional methods for addition and short multiplication, many of the common
errors that children make relate to the 'carries' and so these will not be discussed again here,

although it is worth emphasising that the potentially large number of 'carries' generated in calculations such as these exacerbates the situation.

In addition to 'carries' errors, children commonly forget to write down a zero before multiplying by the tens digit and/or write down a zero when multiplying by the ones digit.

Case Study: Children's multiplication errors

As part of a cross-curricular problem-solving activity, the children in Tony's Year 6 class are planning to turn the playground into a car park for the forthcoming parents' consultation evening. A small group of children are measuring the length and width of the playground and find these to be 83 metres and 24 metres respectively. Tony asks all the children to work out the area of the playground in square metres. Here is part of the discussion that follows.

Tony: So who can tell me the area of the playground then?
(Some children put their hands up)

Tony: OK, Lizzie, what have you got for the answer?

Lizzie: 1612.

Tony: Explain to us how you got that answer.

Lizzie: Well, I partitioned each number, then multiplied 80 by 20 to give 1600, then multiplied 3 by 4 to give 12. 1600 plus 12 is 1612.

Tony: Errr ... I don't think you've quite got that right. I think you ought to try the long multiplication method I showed you earlier. Did anyone do it that way?

Later, when Tony is discussing the calculation with Lizzie, she still cannot understand why her method is giving the wrong answer. At one point she says 'But if I was adding 83 and 24 I'd partition them and add the tens and then add the ones, so why can't I do it for multiplication?' Tony is not able to give an explanation, and so simply tells her to use the traditional pencil and paper method.

Activity

Can you see why Lizzie's method is giving the wrong answer?
How would you explain to Lizzie the flaw in her method?
What visual representation would help Lizzie to understand her misconception?
Which method of multiplication, discussed in Chapter 4, is Lizzie trying to use, but in an incomplete way?

The first important lesson to learn from this case study is that teachers need to have high levels of mathematics subject knowledge in order to diagnose and remedy errors such as this. It is unacceptable to dismiss an incorrect answer and simply tell the child to use an alternative. Lizzie clearly understands place value and is trying to use this, in conjunction with her mental skills, to work out the answer by using an incomplete variation of the 'grid multiplication' method discussed in Chapter 4.

Working out the areas of rectangles is a very good context in which to discuss the grid method because the partitioning of the dimensions relates directly to the dimensions of the smaller rectangles in the resulting grid, and the answers to each separate multiplication correspond to the area of each smaller rectangle, as illustrated below (the dimensions are not drawn to scale).

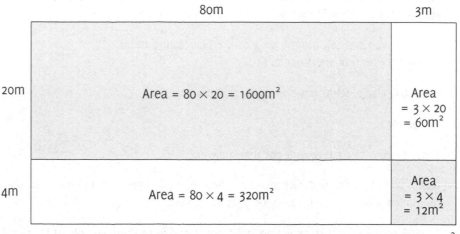

By multiplying only 80 by 30 and 3 by 4 Lizzie has only carried out two of the four multiplications that are necessary. She has worked out the area of the two shaded rectangles above, but needs to also work out the areas of the other two rectangles. A visual image such as this is very powerful when explaining multiplication to children and so it might be better for Tony to pursue this approach with Lizzie, so as to further her understanding, rather than simply insisting that she uses the traditional method of long multiplication.

Case Study

If 'traditional' means 'old' then you cannot get much more traditional than this method because it was used by the Ancient Egyptians. As part of a cross-curricular history topic with her Year 5 class, Jessica introduces the children to Egyptian multiplication. This traditional pencil and paper method is based on doubling and addition. Here is one of the examples that Jessica models for the children (415×26), which just happens to be a calculation you attempted earlier!

$\rightarrow$

415 × 26 =

Write 1 at the left and the bigger number on the right.

Work down, doubling the numbers each time.

1	415
2	830
4	1660
8	3320
16	6640

Stop when the number on the left is more than half of the smaller number in the original multiplication.

Now look for numbers on the left which add up to 26 (16, 8 and 2).

Cross out all of the other rows of numbers.

Add up the remaining numbers on the right (830 + 3320 + 6640 = 10790).

~~1~~	~~415~~
2	830
~~4~~	~~1660~~
8	3320
16	6640

Not all of the children multiply numbers as big as those in the example above, but they all enjoy doing the calculations because they are confident with their doubling and addition.

Traditional methods for division

As with traditional methods for multiplication, the distinction between 'short' and 'long' division depends upon the size of the divisor. Historically, if you are dividing by a number up to 12, this requires a short division method. If you are dividing by a number greater than 12 then this requires long division. The main difference between the two methods is in the way that the remainders are dealt with. For short division, where the remainders are small, they are calculated mentally and are squeezed in front of the next digit to be used in the calculation. For long division, the remainders could be much larger and so they are derived and presented in a more formal way.

Traditional methods for division: short division

When using the traditional method of short division to calculate 809 ÷ 6 it would be set out like this:

6)8 0 9

> ## Activity
>
> Use the traditional method for short division to work out the answer to $809 \div 6$.
>
> Think carefully about the common errors that children might make when tackling this question. Try to list as many errors as possible.

Here is a step-by-step breakdown of the traditional method for short division:

Step 1

$$\begin{array}{r} 1 \\ 6\,\overline{)8\,{}^2 0\ 9} \end{array}$$

In the hundreds column, 8 divided by 6 is 1 remainder 2. Write down the 1 above the line and the remainder 2 in front of the 0.

Step 2

$$\begin{array}{r} 1\ \ 3 \\ 6\,\overline{)8\,{}^2 0\ {}^2 9} \end{array}$$

In the tens column, 20 divided by 6 is 3 remainder 2. Write down the 3 above the line and the remainder 2 in front of the 9.

Step 3

$$\begin{array}{r} 1\ \ 3\ \ 4\ \ \text{r}\,5 \\ 6\,\overline{)8\,{}^2 0\ {}^2 9} \end{array}$$

29 divided by 6 is 4 remainder 5. Write down the 4 above the line and also note the remainder.

Variations

A common variation on the layout presented above looks like this.

$$\begin{array}{l} 6\,\overline{)8\,{}^2 0\ {}^2 9} \\ 1\ \ 3\ \ 4\ \ \text{r}\,5 \end{array}$$

Children's errors in short division

Possible errors that you may have noted include the following.

- Not writing down some or all of the remainders (so in the example above this would give the incorrect answer 101, possibly with a remainder of 3).

- Starting with the ones and working from right to left. So the first step of the calculation would be 9 divided by 6 which is 1 remainder 3. The 1 would be written above the 9 and the remainder written in front of the tens digit. Why do you think a child might work in this way?

Traditional methods for division: long division

When using the traditional method of long division to calculate $953 \div 27$ it would be set out like this:

$$27\,\overline{)9\,5\,3}$$

Activity

Use the traditional method for long division to work out the answer to $953 \div 27$.

Can you see how this method differs from the short division approach?

Here is a step-by-step breakdown of the traditional method for long division:

Step 1

```
        3
2 7 )9 5 3
```

In the hundreds column, 9 divided by 27 is 0. So, 95 tens are divided by 27, which equals 3. Write down the 3 above the line and then calculate the remainder in Step 2, but set out all of the calculations formally, by keeping each digit in the correct column.

Step 2

```
        3
2 7 )9 5 3
    − 8 1
      1 4
```

3 multiplied by 27 is 81. Write down 81 below 95. Subtract 81 from 95 to give the remainder 14.

Step 3

```
       3 5
2 7 )9 5 3
   −  8 1 ↓
      1 4 3
```

Instead of squeezing the remainder (14) in front of the 3, drop the 3 down so that it appears after the 14. 143 divided by 27 equals 5. Write down the 5 above the line and then calculate the remainder in Step 4, again setting out all of the calculations formally.

Step 4

```
       3 5
2 7 )9 5 3
   −  8 1 ↓
      1 4 3
   − 1 3 5
          8
```

5 multiplied by 27 is 135. Write down 135 below 143. Subtract 135 from 143 to give the remainder 8.

The answer is 35 remainder 8.

Comparing the traditional methods for long and short division, the essential difference is in the way we deal with the remainders. With short division the remainders are calculated mentally (because they are never going to be very big) and are squeezed in front of the next digit to be used in the calculation. With long division the remainders are much larger (up to one less than the divisor) and so most people are unable to work these out without writing down the calculations. Additionally, in physical terms it is sometimes difficult to squeeze a two-digit remainder in front of the next digit to be used.

Implications for your teaching

Many of the important implications have already been considered towards the beginning of this chapter in the section 'So where does that leave the teacher?' and consequently they will not be discussed again in detail here. However, by way of summary, it is worth reiterating the following points. You should resist the temptation to introduce the traditional written methods too soon in children's arithmetical development, and should wait until they are ready for them. These methods are the final stage in the line of progression, but that does not mean that they are necessarily better than what has gone before, and so you should never suggest to children that they should use traditional arithmetic at the expense of mental methods. Even when you do introduce traditional arithmetic you should at least attempt to achieve some degree of relational understanding among the children. The contrast between relational understanding and instrumental understanding (sometimes referred to as procedural fluency) is considered in the Research Focus in Chapter 1 and so you might like to revisit it. The final implication relates to addressing children's errors when using traditional arithmetic. Always establish the specific nature of the error so that targeted intervention can be provided on an individual basis. Simply modelling the procedure repeatedly to the whole class, and asking children to do more of the same in the hope that they will eventually get it right, is unlikely to be a successful strategy.

Learning Outcomes Review

You should now be aware of the government's expectations regarding *quick, efficient written methods of calculation* (DfE, 2012a) and be able to make an informed judgement as to how this relates to the teaching of traditional pencil and paper arithmetic. The traditional methods provide, for some children, a compact, quick and efficient way of dealing with a particular calculation, but they should never be held up as always being the 'correct' or 'best' way.

This chapter should have equipped you with the subject knowledge and understanding to utilise all of the traditional methods yourself and also to model them for your children. However, as a teacher you must go beyond simply being able to follow the rules and procedures; you also need to have an insight into how these compact and efficient algorithms actually work. This will contribute to the overall development of your own mathematics subject knowledge, but also enable you to diagnose and remedy children's errors more effectively. If children repeatedly make mistakes when using the traditional algorithms there is little point in simply giving them more of the same in the hope that eventually they will get it right. You must identify the nature of the error or misconception and provide specific, targeted intervention to address it, rather than simply marking the answer as being wrong and asking the children to try another one.

You should now have an appreciation of where the traditional pencil and paper methods stand in relation to the other modes of arithmetic that have been discussed in Chapters 2, 3 and 4. The traditional methods should be viewed as an endpoint in children's progression, which they should all eventually reach, although for some children this journey may have to continue beyond their primary school years. When this endpoint has been reached, however, this does not mean that mental methods should diminish in status. As discussed in Chapter 3, children should always consider mental arithmetic as the first resort, and this principle should be afforded particular attention once traditional written methods are introduced. One important implication to be aware of in relation to this is never to insist that children use a traditional pencil and paper method if they are capable of working out the answer mentally. Such insistence is not uncommon amongst primary teachers who mistakenly tell children to 'always show your working out' and feel it necessary for them to calculate something like 301 − 198 using traditional methods, just so that they know how to cope with the exchanging when there is a zero in the bigger number. These practices undermine the status of mental methods and ultimately lead to children using traditional pencil and paper arithmetic when in fact a quicker, more efficient alternative is available.

One final thing to consider in relation to children's progression in their approaches to arithmetic is the role of calculators. Even if children are fully competent in using traditional pencil and paper methods, there is little point in expecting them to use these methods for large numbers or for complex calculations. In such cases it is wholly appropriate to use a calculator. The role of the traditional written methods in relation to that of calculators has been considered by many educational commentators over the last forty years and the gist of the argument is perhaps best summed up by Plunkett, who stated that:

> The advent of calculators has provided us with a great opportunity. We are freed from the necessity to provide every citizen with methods for dealing with calculations of indefinite complexity. So we can abandon the standard written algorithms, of general applicability and limited intelligibility, in favour of methods more suited to the minds and purposes of the users.
>
> (Plunkett, 1979, page 5)

The use of calculators for arithmetic in primary schools is discussed in greater detail in Chapter 7.

Self-assessment questions
Answer the following questions using the traditional compact pencil and paper methods that have been discussed in this chapter.
1. 714 − 368
2. 837 + 588
3. 43 × 517
4. 1049 ÷ 37 (use remainders rather than decimals)

Now look back on your attempts at the self-assessment questions at the end of Chapter 4. Had you spotted the similarity? So which methods did you feel most comfortable with: the traditional ones you've just used or the expanded, informal methods that you used earlier?

Further Reading

Hansen, A. (ed) (2011) *Children's Errors in Mathematics* (2nd edition) London: Learning Matters. In particular have a look at section 8 of Chapter 3 ('The four rules of arithmetic').

O'Sullivan, L., Harris, A., Sangster, M., Wild, J., Donaldson, G. and Bottle, G. (2005) *Primary Mathematics: Reflective Reader*. London: Learning Matters. Read Chapter 4 ('Mental and written calculation strategies').

References

Boulton-Lewis, G.M. (1998) 'Children's Strategy Use and Interpretations of Mathematical Representations', *Journal of Mathematical Behavior*, 17 (2): 219–37.

DfE (2012a) *Key priorities for arithmetic*. Presentation to ITT mathematics tutors, TDA/UCET/NASBTT conference for Primary ITT tutors, Lancaster and London. March, 2012.

DfE (2012b) *National Curriculum for Mathematics: Key Stages 1 and 2 – Draft*. London: DfE Publications.

Hart, K. (1987) 'Children's Mathematical Frameworks: Part Three Subtraction', *Mathematics in School*, 16 (5): 30–33.

Houssart, J. (2000) 'The Role of Number Resources in the Daily Mathematics Lesson', *Proceedings of the British Society for Research into Learning Mathematics*, 20 (3): 37–42.

McNeil, N.M. and Jarvin, L. (2007) 'When Theories Don't Add Up: Disentangling the Manipulatives Debate', *Theory into Practice*, 46 (4): 309–16.

O'Sullivan, L., Harris, A., Sangster, M., Wild, J., Donaldson, G. and Bottle, G. (2005) *Primary Mathematics: Reflective Reader*. London: Learning Matters.

Plunkett, S. (1979) 'Decomposition and all that rot', *Mathematics in School*, 8 (3): 2–5.

Thompson, I. (2009) 'Place value?' *Mathematics Teaching*, 215: 4–5.

Thompson, I. and Bramald, R. (2002) *An investigation of the relationship between young children's understanding of place value and their competence at mental addition*. Final report submitted to the Nuffield Foundation. Newcastle: Department of Education, University of Newcastle upon Tyne.

6. Arithmetic with fractions, decimals, percentages and ratios

Learning Outcomes

By the end of this chapter you will:
- be aware of the curriculum expectations in relation to arithmetic involving fractions, decimals, percentages and ratios in primary schools;
- appreciate the understanding required before these aspects of arithmetic can be introduced to children;
- be able to use a range of efficient mental and written methods to calculate using fractions, decimals, percentages and ratios, based on those introduced in Chapters 3, 4 and 5;
- understand some of the limitations of traditional algorithms for calculating with fractions, decimals and percentages.

Introduction

The arithmetic that children and adults are expected to carry out as part of their everyday lives is not restricted to whole numbers and so this chapter will explore some of the issues associated with calculations involving fractions, decimals, percentages and ratios. You will see how in some cases the principles and strategies discussed in earlier chapters can be adapted and used with these types of numbers, but additionally there are some techniques which are very specific to them, hence the need for a separate chapter.

The aim of this chapter is not to provide a comprehensive discussion of all the subject and pedagogical knowledge relating to fractions, decimals, percentages and ratios. Instead, the focus will be on approaches to arithmetic involving these types of numbers and so much of the content mentioned in the 'Laying the foundations' section below will have to be explored in greater depth using alternative sources, if you feel that this is necessary. The Further Reading section at the end of this chapter provides a list of possible sources for you to consult.

What do children need to know?

It is important that curriculum expectations reflect the realities that children and adults will be faced with in their everyday lives. Since 1988 the statutory requirements for mathematics and the associated non-statutory guidance, such as that provided by the National Numeracy Strategy and the National Strategies, have generally presented a realistic and balanced view of what children should be capable of doing by the time they leave primary school. So, for example, children have not been expected to carry out complex arithmetic involving fractions such as $2\frac{3}{4} \times 1\frac{2}{5}$, although in the not so dim and distant past this was the sort of arithmetic that was taught before the age of 11. You only have to ask yourself the question 'When was the last time I had to carry out a calculation like this?' to appreciate that it makes little sense at all to expect this of children in primary schools, because it would not reflect the demands of the real world in which we live. Instead, primary teachers should be ensuring that children fully understand the concept of fractions and are able to use and apply this in everyday situations. Similarly with decimals, we would expect many children, by the time they leave primary school, to be able to carry out some simple decimal calculations mentally, and more complex ones using written methods, but it would be wholly inappropriate to require a child to work out 12.483×7.625 without access to a calculator.

As stated earlier in this section, the curriculum requirements over the past 25 years have, on the whole, been realistic in their expectations in relation to fractions, decimals, percentages and ratios. However, the recently published draft programmes of study for mathematics (DfE, 2012) indicate a possible change of emphasis in the future, particularly with regard to fractions, as illustrated by the following extracts:

- add and subtract fractions with the same denominator (Year 5);
- multiply proper fractions and mixed numbers by whole numbers (Year 5);
- add and subtract mixed numbers and fractions with different denominators (Year 6);
- multiply simple unit fractions by fractions and pairs of proper fractions, writing the answer in its simplest form (Year 6);
- divide proper fractions by whole numbers (Year 6).

If these proposals remain in the final version of the programmes of study, they will represent a raising of expectations in terms of what children should be taught by the time they leave primary school.

While acknowledging the draft proposals presented above and touching on some of the related content, this chapter will focus on the subject knowledge associated with the arithmetic that primary-aged children are currently expected to engage with which, in the main, relates to everyday contexts. So if you really do want to know how to work out $2\frac{3}{4} \times 1\frac{2}{5}$ you will have to look elsewhere!

Laying the foundations for arithmetic with fractions, decimals, percentages and ratios

Because the focus of this chapter is very much on the arithmetic associated with fractions, decimals, percentages and ratios, it will not consider the early stages in the teaching of these areas, during which children will be introduced to key concepts, terminology and skills. If you would like to find out more about these stages of children's progression then please consult the

Further Reading section at the end of this chapter. However, the prerequisites, which provide the foundations for arithmetic, are identified below.

Fractions

Children need to understand the concept of a fraction in terms of its being 'part of a whole one' and from the outset the notion of 'equal parts' must be introduced and constantly reinforced, because this underpins all of the later work. Once the formal notation for fractions has been introduced, children will need to understand the terms 'numerator' and 'denominator', and again this needs to be linked to the number of equal parts in the whole. Children should encounter a range of fractions with different denominators and also be able to identify and create equivalent fractions by using a 'multiplier' or 'scaling up' effect. Equivalent fractions can also be produced by 'scaling down' or dividing, a process more commonly referred to as 'cancelling down'. Once children understand equivalent fractions they should be able to compare and order fractions by first ensuring that they all have the same denominator, called the 'common denominator'.

Research Focus: Why do children struggle with fractions?

Keiren (1976) was one of the first authors to point out that fractions are not a single concept for children to understand, but instead comprise five different components or interpretations. The first of these is the 'part-whole' component, whereby a whole object is divided into equal parts and some are selected. This is the way that most children first encounter fractions, for example in relation to three-quarters of a cake. The second is the 'quotient' component, which relates to the division of whole number quantities to produce fractions, for example when 3 pizzas are shared equally between 4 people to produce the answer ¾. The third is the 'ratio' component, in which fractions are used to compare the relative sizes of two objects, for example where one length of ribbon is three-quarters of the length of another. The 'measure' component is usually associated with the marking of fractions on number lines, thus providing a possible way of considering the addition and subtraction of fractions. The 'operator' component utilises fractions in a multiplicative sense, for example by calculating three-quarters of 15 objects.

It is the multi-faceted nature of fractions that makes it a difficult concept for children to understand and it is therefore vitally important that teachers employ an appropriate range of contexts, structures, models and images.

Keiren's classification has been used by many authors as the basis of their research and instruction relating to fractions and so you might like to refer to Chapter 2 of Mooney et al. (2011) for a more detailed discussion of this.

Decimals

Children first encounter decimals in the context of money, where the decimal point is used to separate the pounds from the pence. This link with measures should be continued throughout Key Stage 2, because it provides an excellent context for just about any work involving measures. If we want children to understand and use decimal notation then it is vitally important that they have a firm grasp of the place value aspects. Many teachers try to push children too quickly on to calculating with decimals without laying the necessary foundations relating to place value. If a child is still recognising 0.25 as 'nought point twenty-five' and thinks that this is bigger than 'nought point seven' (because 25 is bigger than 7) then there is little point in attempting to move on to arithmetic. The misconceptions relating to place value must be resolved first. Children will need lots of practice at reading, writing, comparing and ordering decimals before attempting any arithmetic. Another aspect of decimals which older children will need to understand, particularly when making links with fractions, is the notion of recurring decimals.

Percentages

When children are introduced to percentages later in the primary school, this should be viewed as a natural extension of the work on fractions, because that is precisely what a percentage is – a fraction with a denominator of 100, that is, there are 100 equal parts. Percentage notation should therefore be thought of as a shorthand way of writing 'hundredths'. Other ways of thinking of percentages are therefore 'parts per hundred' and 'pennies in every pound'.

Equivalent forms of fractions, decimals and percentages

Because fractions, decimals and percentages each provide a way of expressing part of a whole, they can be used interchangeably. So, for example, $\frac{2}{5}$ of the children in your class might be boys, which can also be written as 0.4 and 40%. As children develop their knowledge and understanding of fractions and decimals, the equivalences between them should be discussed and later this should be expanded to include percentages. By the end of Key Stage 2 many children should know as number facts many of the simple equivalences between the three forms, for example that $\frac{3}{4}$ is equivalent to 0.75 and 75%. Other equivalences can be worked out quickly using the ones that are already known. For example, if children know that $\frac{1}{4}$ is 25% then they can quickly deduce that $\frac{1}{8}$, which is half of $\frac{1}{4}$, must be half of 25%, that is, 12.5%. Similarly, knowing that $\frac{1}{8}$ is 12.5% can be used to quickly work out that $\frac{3}{8}$ is 37.5% and that $\frac{5}{8}$ is 62.5%. For more complex conversions between fractions, decimals and percentages it is appropriate to use a calculator. So, for example, if in a survey of 93 people, 59 of them eat breakfast, we can say that:

$\frac{59}{93}$ of the sample eats breakfast
0.634 of the sample eats breakfast   (divide numerator by denominator)
63.4% of the sample eats breakfast   (multiply the decimal equivalent by 100)
(Rounded to 3 significant figures.)

Ratios

In the upper primary years children should be introduced to the concept of ratios and the associated notation. The key facet of a ratio is that it provides a way of identifying and comparing the parts that make up a whole, although this is not the only way in which ratios can be utilised. A useful expression to use is 'for every', as in 'there are 3 girls for every 4 boys'. In order to use ratios effectively in their calculations, children will need to understand the concept of equivalent ratios, which can be created by using a 'scaling up' or 'scaling down' effect similar to that mentioned above in relation to equivalent fractions.

Ratio and proportion

The expression 'proportion' is one which is often used when considering fractions, decimals, percentages and ratio and so its meaning needs to be clarified. A ratio, as discussed above, provides a way of comparing the parts that make up a whole. For example, to make concrete you mix 5 parts sand, to every 3 parts cement to every 2 parts gravel. This could be represented using the following notation.

$$\text{Sand} \; : \; \text{Cement} \; : \; \text{Gravel}$$
$$5 \; : \; 3 \; : \; 2$$

Whereas the ratio 5:3:2 compares the parts that make up the whole, a proportion compares each of the parts with the whole. These proportions can be expressed as fractions, decimals or percentages. So, in the example above, we can see that 0.5 of the concrete mix is sand, $\frac{3}{10}$ is cement and 20% is gravel.

The importance of models and images

When laying the foundations presented above it is crucially important that appropriate models and images are used. So, for example, when considering equivalent fractions, use three identical rectangular strips divided into thirds, quarters and twelfths respectively, to illustrate that two-thirds is equivalent to eighth-twelfths and that three-quarters is equivalent to nine-twelfths. The visual image is a powerful one which enhances what would otherwise be a very abstract concept, presented purely in symbolic form. Interactive whiteboard software can be utilised to present these sorts of images to whole classes of children. Similarly, for decimals a number line is an effective visual aid to use. It is also possible to make or purchase decimal place value cards to emphasise this important aspect of the work. For percentages use large images which have been divided into one hundred equal parts, and for ratio work display sets of counters or other objects to demonstrate equivalent ratios. These are just a few examples of models and images that can be used to develop children's understanding of fractions, decimals, percentages and ratios, and these continue to have a vital role when children start to encounter arithmetic, as we shall see later in this chapter.

Case Study: Children's misconceptions when working with fractions

Steve has been spending a few lessons with his Year 6 class looking at equivalent fractions and the ordering of fractions by making use of common denominators, in conjunction with visual representations on the interactive whiteboard. In the plenary of today's lesson he is assessing how much they have learned and so asks them to find a fraction between ½ and ⅘, by first discussing this in pairs. He represents the two fractions on the interactive whiteboard as two shaded rectangular strips to assist the children's discussions. Here is an extract from the conversation he has with the children.

Steve: So, who has managed to find one for me?
OK, Sam, what have you and Misha come up with?

Sam: ¾, sir.
[Steve represents ¾ as another shaded rectangular strip and places it between the two existing ones, as shown below]

Steve:
So we can see from our fractions wall that ¾ is bigger than ½ but smaller than ¾. Well done both of you!

Steve: So, Misha, how did you and Sam come up with ¾? What did you discuss together.

Misha: Well, first we looked at the numerators and picked a number between 1 and 4, and then we looked at the denominators and picked a number between 2 and 5.

Steve: That's excellent, well done!
Can anyone else use Misha and Sam's method to give me another fraction between ½ and ⅘?

Ben: ⅔ should work because 2 is between 1 and 4 and 3 is between 2 and 5.

> ## Activity
>
> Study Sam and Misha's method carefully.
>
> Construct a fractions wall of your own, like the one shown above, and insert a rectangular strip for $\frac{2}{3}$ so that all four fractions are in order of size.
>
> Is Sam and Misha's method a sound one or is it flawed?
>
> Use their method to find fractions between $\frac{1}{2}$ and $\frac{7}{10}$.
>
> What conclusions can you make?

Sam and Misha's method does work for $\frac{1}{2}$, $\frac{3}{4}$ and $\frac{4}{5}$. Indeed, if you include $\frac{2}{3}$ in the list it should appear between $\frac{1}{2}$ and $\frac{3}{4}$ and so numerically fits the rule they have proposed. However, this is purely by chance because if you attempt the same method with, for example, $\frac{1}{2}$, $\frac{3}{4}$ and $\frac{7}{10}$ it does not work, since $\frac{3}{4}$ is in fact bigger than $\frac{7}{10}$. Similarly, the fractions $\frac{4}{5}$ and $\frac{5}{6}$ should, according to Sam and Misha's method, be between $\frac{1}{2}$ and $\frac{7}{10}$ but they are both bigger than $\frac{7}{10}$.

There are two important lessons to be learned from this case study. Firstly, you need to ensure that you have the necessary mathematics subject knowledge to understand the explanations that children offer. Without this, you will not be able to identify children's errors and misconceptions, let alone rectify them. Secondly, you must be wary of children (and possibly yourself) making false generalisations based on one particular case that apparently demonstrates a particular pattern or relationship. Another common example of this, relevant to this chapter, is the relationship between fractions and percentages. Children know that $\frac{1}{10}$ is 10% and so falsely assume that $\frac{1}{8}$ is 8%, $\frac{1}{20}$ is 20%, and so on.

Arithmetic with fractions

Creating fractions from a presented scenario

Probably the simplest type of calculation that children have to deal with involving fractions is usually based around a scenario or visual image from which a fraction has to be derived. Two typical examples are presented below.

1. In a class there are 12 boys and 18 girls. What fraction of the class is boys?

2. What fraction of this grid is shaded?

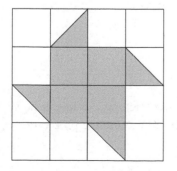

These sorts of examples require children to understand the basic concept and definition of a fraction, in particular the identification of 'the whole'. In the second example 'the whole', that is, the 16 squares in the grid, is perhaps more obvious than in the first example, where some children might incorrectly give the answer $^{12}/_{18}$ or a simplified equivalent such as $^2/_3$.

Fractions problems involving addition, subtraction, multiplication and division

The traditional written algorithms for adding, subtracting, multiplying and dividing fractions have been in use for many years, but these are certainly not the only ways of tackling fractions problems, as we shall see in this section.

Activity

Work out the answers to each of the following questions. You can use any method you want but must not use a calculator. Feel free to use any combination of mental methods, traditional pencil and paper methods, informal jottings and diagrams, etc. If you use a mental method, make brief notes to indicate how you actually calculated the answer.

1. A jogger runs $3\frac{1}{2}$ miles on Saturday and $4\frac{3}{4}$ miles on Sunday. How far did he run altogether?
2. Here's a rhyme for converting litres into pints: *A litre of water's a pint and three-quarters.* How many pints are there in 3 litres?
3. 3 people share $2\frac{1}{2}$ pizzas equally between them. How much pizza does each person get?
4. A person uses $^3/_5$ of a pint of milk each day. How long will a 4-pint container of milk last? How much milk is left over as the final portion?

Question 1

Let's start by tackling this fractions addition problem by using the traditional pencil and paper method that children are likely to encounter during Key Stage 3, although it is not many years ago that this procedure was introduced during the primary phase.

$$3\tfrac{1}{2} + 4\tfrac{3}{4} = 3\tfrac{2}{4} + 4\tfrac{3}{4}$$

(Convert $\frac{1}{2}$ to the equivalent fraction $^2/_4$ so that it can be added to $^3/_4$.)

$$= 7\tfrac{2+3}{4}$$
$$= 7\tfrac{5}{4}$$
$$= 8\tfrac{1}{4}$$

This method can be applied to the addition and subtraction of any fractions, no matter how complex, although its success is dependent upon children's ability to execute the procedure accurately. The identification of a common denominator (4 in the example above) is crucial, but is often the source of many children's errors.

One of the disadvantages of the traditional pencil and paper method is that it is unnecessarily complex when dealing with certain fractions which can be juggled mentally. It is possible that you tackled this question by simply adding the 3 and 4 and then adding $\frac{1}{2}$ and $\frac{1}{4}$, but managed to do all of this mentally. Many children by the end of Key Stage 2 should be capable of mentally adding simple fractions such as $\frac{1}{2}$ and $\frac{3}{4}$. If necessary, provide children with models and images or contexts that they can relate to. For example, you could talk in terms of half an hour plus three-quarters of an hour, or represent the two fractions as shaded parts of rectangular strips or circles.

Question 2

Again, let's start by using the traditional pencil and paper method for fractions multiplication.

$$1\tfrac{3}{4} \times 3 = \tfrac{7}{4} \times \tfrac{3}{1}$$

(Convert $1\frac{3}{4}$ and 3 from mixed/whole numbers into improper fractions.)

$$= \tfrac{21}{4}$$

(Multiply the numerators to give 21 and the denominators to give 4.)

$$= 5\tfrac{1}{4}$$

(Convert the improper fraction into mixed number.)

With lots of practice, children can carry out this procedure competently, but as with the traditional method for addition, it is sometimes unnecessarily complex. An alternative approach, based on mental methods, but possibly with the aid of some jottings, would be to work out 3 lots of $\frac{3}{4}$ and then add the 3 whole pints. Three lots of $\frac{3}{1}$ could be thought of as multiplication, using appropriate concrete or mental images, to produce the answer $\frac{9}{4}$ which is $2\frac{1}{4}$. It could also be thought of as repeated addition, that is, $\frac{3}{4} + \frac{3}{4} + \frac{3}{4}$. This might again give the answer $\frac{9}{4}$, but it could also be tackled by thinking '$\frac{3}{4}$ plus $\frac{3}{4}$ is $1\frac{1}{2}$. Add another $\frac{3}{4}$ and that makes $2\frac{1}{4}$.' The key point here is that the mental approach, possibly with jottings, and supported by appropriate models and images, is based on children's understanding of fractions, whereas the traditional methods are sets of rules to be followed blindly, without any understanding of the processes involved.

Question 3

If you thought the traditional pencil and paper method for multiplication was complicated, let's see what you think about the division algorithm.

$$2\tfrac{1}{2} \div 3 = \tfrac{5}{2} \div \tfrac{3}{1}$$

(Convert $2\frac{1}{2}$ and 3 from mixed/whole numbers into improper fractions.)

$= \frac{5}{2} \times \frac{1}{3}$

(Change the division to multiplication and invert the second fraction.)

$= \frac{5}{6}$

(Multiply the numerators to give 5 and the denominators to give 6.)

This method will always generate correct answers if the procedure is followed accurately, regardless of the numbers involved, but yet again children are following rules blindly rather than making use of their understanding of fractions. Why does a division become a multiplication and why is the second fraction turned upside down? Children don't need to know why – they just have to follow the rules! However, it is hoped that you understand why these things happen, using your understanding of inverse operations and equivalence. Essentially, division by any number is equivalent to multiplication by its *reciprocal*. Using the example above, division by 3 is equivalent to multiplication by ⅓. Similarly, division by ⅕ is equivalent to multiplication by 5 (think it terms of 'how many fifths can I get from ...'). This is discussed further when considering question 4 below.

So what are the alternatives to the traditional fractions division algorithm? Instead of trying to remember rules all you have to do is think carefully about the situation being presented, create appropriate models and images, and use your knowledge and understanding of fractions. Here are the 2½ pizzas that are to be shared between the three people.

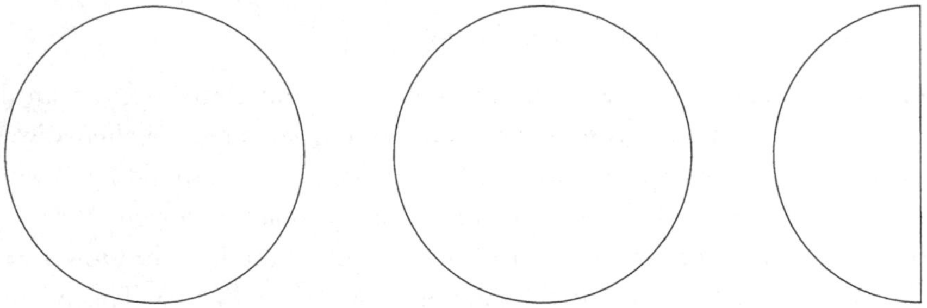

The usual way to share a pizza is to divide it into six equal parts (sixths). This is a good choice when sharing pizza between three people, because each person gets ²⁄₆ of each pizza. The half pizza consists of ³⁄₆, so that's another piece for each person. Each person therefore gets 5 pieces of pizza, that is, ⅚ of a pizza, as shown below.

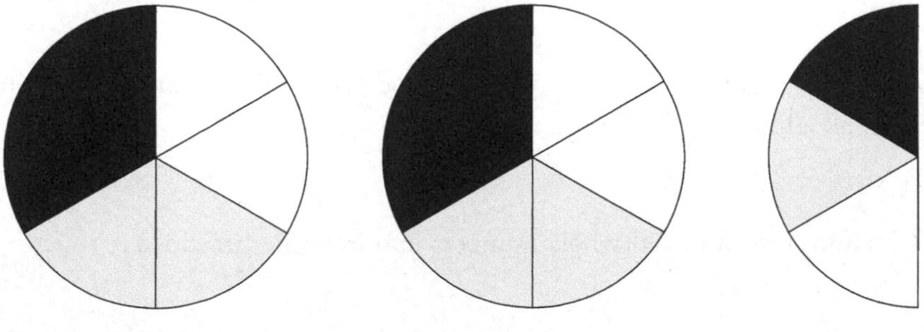

Another way of thinking of it is that each person initially gets half a pizza, which uses up 1½ pizzas. The remaining pizza is divided into three equal parts (thirds) and each person gets one of them. So each person gets a half and a third, which, if you think in terms of sixths (a common denominator), is ⅚ of a pizza, as shown below.

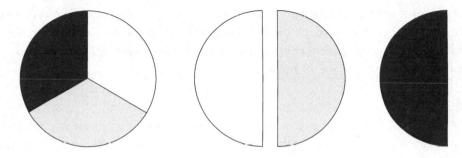

Question 4

As always, let's start by looking at the traditional approach to finding how many times ⅗ will go into 4 by using the division algorithm.

$$4 \div \frac{3}{5} = \frac{4}{1} \div \frac{3}{5}$$

(Convert 4 from a whole number into an improper fraction.)

$$= \frac{4}{1} \times \frac{5}{3}$$

(Change the division to multiplication and invert the second fraction.)

$$= \frac{20}{3}$$

(Multiply the numerators to give 20 and the denominators to give 3.)

$$= 6\frac{2}{3}$$

Yet again we have an unnecessarily complex calculation, but even if you are able to execute it accurately there is the additional hurdle of being able to make sense of the answer. We were trying to find out how many times ⅗ would go into 4. The answer above indicates that it will go 6⅔ times, so that's six portions of milk, but what does the ⅔ represent? Is this telling us that there is ⅔ of a pint of milk left in the container? Well actually, no it is not. It is in fact telling us that ⅔ of a portion is left over, so that's ⅔ of a ⅗ pint portion, which means there is ⅖ of a pint in the container. Can you appreciate how the traditional algorithm has made this problem incredibly complicated, when a far more reliable and efficient alternative can be used?

Why not think of the problem as repeated subtraction because that is precisely what happens in real terms – ⅗ of a pint is removed from the container each day. Four full pints can be thought of as being ²⁰⁄₅, so if ⅗ are removed each day, that's 6 portions of milk (¹⁸⁄₅), leaving ⅖ in the container. It really is that simple, but sadly many children would be directed towards the traditional division algorithm when faced with that particular question, although this is likely to be an issue in secondary rather than primary schools.

Fractional parts

Much of the arithmetic described above is not typical of what we encounter in our everyday lives. However, one context in which fractions do crop up is on the high street when the sales are in full swing and goods have been discounted by a fractional amount. Here are two fractional parts questions for you to attempt.

Activity

Work out the answers to each of the following questions. You can use any method you want but must not use a calculator. Feel free to use any combination of mental methods, traditional pencil and paper methods, informal jottings and diagrams, etc. If you use a mental method, make brief notes to indicate how you actually calculated the answer.

1. A coat costs £48 but there is '$\frac{1}{3}$ off!' in the sale. What is the sale price?
2. $\frac{5}{8}$ of the 72 students in my lecture don't understand fractions. How many students is this?

In the past, the recommended approach for tackling questions such as these was to think of them as fractions multiplications using the traditional algorithm, as illustrated below.

$$48 \times \frac{2}{3} = \frac{48}{1} \times \frac{2}{3}$$

$$72 \times \frac{5}{8} = \frac{72}{1} \times \frac{5}{8}$$

As discussed earlier in this chapter, these approaches do children no favours at all because they are based on remembering rules rather than on understanding, and the success of the algorithm is dependent upon the children's ability to execute it accurately. If children understand fractions then instead of the traditional algorithm they should be using a 'common sense' approach, as explained below.

Question 1: $\frac{1}{3}$ of £48

If I understand the relationship between fractions and division I should know that to find $\frac{1}{3}$ of something I must divide by 3, which can be done mentally. So $\frac{1}{3}$ of £48 is £16 and the sale price is therefore £32.

Question 2: $\frac{5}{8}$ of 72 students

Find $\frac{1}{8}$ by dividing by 8, to give 9. So $\frac{5}{8}$ of 72 students is $5 \times 9 = 45$ students.

Research Focus: Fractions 'problems' and fractions 'computations'

Hart (1981) carried out extensive research in the late 1970s involving several hundred children in the first four years of their secondary school education. As part of this research the children attempted fractions 'problems' and, on a separate occasion, fractions 'computations' which were aligned with the problems that had been attempted earlier. Here is an example of a 'problem' and the corresponding 'computation'.

Problem: Shade in ⅙ of the grey section of the circle. What fraction of the whole circle have you shaded?

Computation: ⅙ of ¾ = ...

Hart concludes that:

> *There appeared to be no connection in many children's minds between the problem and the 'sum' since they could successfully deal with the problem but could not apply the same method to the computation. It was as if two completely different types of mathematics were involved, one where the children could use common sense, the other where they had to remember a rule.*

And that:

> *The ability to solve computations declines as the child gets older. The ability to solve problems does not decrease with age and one is left with the hypothesis that the problems are solved without recourse to the computational algorithms. Many children do not in fact seem to connect the algorithms with the problem solving and use their own methods.*

Arithmetic with decimals

Children are more likely to encounter calculations involving decimals than fractions and so it is important that their arithmetical skills are of a high standard. However, this does not imply that only the traditional algorithms can be used. All of the approaches to arithmetic discussed throughout this book can be utilised when calculating with decimals, as we shall see in this section.

> ## Activity
> Work out the answers to each of the following questions. You can use any method you want but must not use a calculator. Feel free to use any combination of mental methods, traditional pencil and paper methods, informal jottings and diagrams, etc. If you use a mental method, make brief notes to indicate how you actually calculated the answer.
>
> 1. 3.75 + 1.3
> 2. 4.1 − 1.95
> 3. 17.9 × 4
> 4. 13.5 ÷ 0.25

Here are some possible ways that each of the questions could have been answered using mental, informal written and traditional written methods. The approaches you used, or something similar, might be among those presented below. Study the possibilities carefully and make sure you understand what is being illustrated in each case. Detailed step-by-step explanations have not been included because these have been provided in earlier chapters. So, for example, if you require a detailed explanation of subtraction by decomposition, please refer back to Chapter 5.

Question 1: 3.75 + 1.3
Possible mental approaches, based on those discussed in Chapter 3, include the following.

- Partition the two numbers and then work out 3 + 1 and 0.7 + 0.3. Add the answers to give 5 and then finally add 0.05.

- Round 3.75 up to 4, add this to 1.3 (5.3) and finally subtract 0.25 to compensate for the original rounding up.

- Think in terms of money, i.e. the calculation becomes £3.75 + £1.30, thus making the decimal aspect more accessible. (How might you actually work this out though?)

Informal pencil and paper approaches, based on those discussed in Chapter 4, include the following.

- Use an expanded horizontal method, based on partitioning:
$$3.75 + 1.3 = (3 + 0.7 + 0.05) + (1 + 0.3)$$
$$= 4 + 1.0 + 0.05$$
$$= 5.05$$

- Use an expanded vertical method:

$$
\begin{array}{r}
3.75 \\
+ \ \underline{1.3} \\
4 \\
1.0 \\
\underline{0.05} \\
\underline{5.05}
\end{array}
$$

The traditional pencil and paper approach, discussed in Chapter 5, is presented below. The vital teaching point is that the decimal points must be vertically aligned so that tenths are added to tenths, hundredths are added to hundredths, and so on. Any 'gaps' can, if you wish, be filled with zeros, so that, for example, 1.3 is written as 1.30.

$$
\begin{array}{r}
3.75 \\
+\ 1_{1}.30 \\
\hline
5.05
\end{array}
$$

Question 2: 4.1 − 1.95

Possible mental approaches, based on those discussed in Chapter 3, include the following.

- Round 1.95 up to 2, subtract this from 4.1 (2.1) and finally add back 0.05 to compensate for the original rounding up.

- Think in terms of difference and so count on from 1.95 to 4.1 or count back from 4.1 to 1.95.

- Think in terms of money, i.e. the calculation becomes £4.10 − £1.95, thus making the decimal aspect more accessible. (How might you actually work this out though?)

Informal pencil and paper approaches, based on those discussed in Chapter 4, include the following.

- Think in terms of difference and so use an ENL to count from the lower to the higher number.

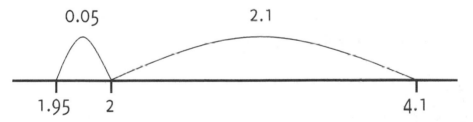

- Use complementary addition but without the ENL.

4.1 − 1.95 =
1.95
  (+ 0.05)
2
  (+ 2)
4
  (+ 0.1)
4.1
  (Total 2.15)

The traditional pencil and paper approach using decomposition, discussed in Chapter 5, is presented below. As with addition, the decimal points must be vertically aligned and any 'gaps' can be filled with zeros, so that, for example, 4.1 is written as 4.10.

$$
\begin{array}{r}
{}^{3}\!\!\not{4} \;.\; {}^{10}\!\!\not{\!1}\; {}^{1}0 \\
-\;\; 1 \;.\; 9 \;\; 5 \\
\hline
2 \;.\; 1 \;\; 5
\end{array}
$$

Question 3: 17.9 × 4

Possible mental approaches, based on those discussed in Chapter 3, include the following.

- Partition 17.9 and then work out $17 \times 4 = 68$ and $0.9 \times 4 = 3.6$ and finally add these two answers.

- Round 17.9 up to 18, work out 18×4 (72) and then subtract four lots of 0.1 (0.4) to compensate for the original rounding up.

- Repeated doubling, i.e. 17.9, 35.8, 71.6.

Informal pencil and paper approaches, based on those discussed in Chapter 4, include the following.

- Use an expanded horizontal method, based on the distribution of multiplication over addition.

$$
\begin{aligned}
4 \times 17.9 &= 4 \times (10 + 7 + 0.9) \\
&= 40 + 28 + 3.6 \\
&= 71.6
\end{aligned}
$$

- Use an expanded vertical method.

$$
\begin{array}{r}
17.9 \\
\times \;\; 4 \\
\hline
40 \\
28 \\
+ \;\; 3.6 \\
\hline
71.6
\end{array}
$$

- Use an expanded method (horizontal or vertical), based on the distribution of multiplication over subtraction.

$$
\begin{aligned}
4 \times 17.9 &= 4 \times (18 - 0.1) \\
&= 72 - 0.4 \\
&= 71.6
\end{aligned}
$$

- Use the grid method.

×	4
10	40
7	28
0.9	3.6
	71.6

The traditional pencil and paper approach using short multiplication, discussed in Chapter 5, is presented below. It is not necessary for the decimal points to be vertically aligned, as is the case with decimal addition and subtraction. So, in the example below, the 4 ones and 7 ones are not aligned. The multiplication is carried out ignoring any decimal points.

$$
\begin{array}{r}
1\,7.9 \\
\times \quad {}_{3}\,{}_{3}\,4 \\
\hline
7\,1\,6
\end{array}
$$

When the numerical answer has been worked out, the decimal point has to be inserted in the appropriate place. There are rules in common use to assist this process, for example 'There must be the same number of digits after the decimal point in the answer as in the question' – one digit in this example so the answer is 71.6. But do you know why this rule works? By ignoring the decimal point in 17.9 you are, in effect, multiplying it by 10 to become 179. The product is therefore 10 times bigger than it should be and so you must divide 716 by 10 to give 71.6 as the final answer. Having said all of that, a much better alternative is to encourage children to use their estimation skills to decide where the decimal point should go. We know that 4×18 is 72, so the answer must be 71.6 and it cannot possibly be 716 or 0.716.

Question 4: 13.5 ÷ 0.25

Possible mental approaches, based on those discussed in Chapter 3, include the following.

- Utilise the inverse relationship between multiplication and division, and therefore think in terms of 'What do I multiply 0.25 by to get 13.5?'
- Consider division as grouping, and therefore think of it as 'How many lots of 0.25 can I get from 13.5?' There are 4 lots of 0.25 in 1, so that's 52 lots in 13, plus another 2 lots in 0.5, making 54 lots altogether.
- Recognise that $13.5 \div 0.25$ and $1350 \div 25$ are equivalent calculations which produce the same answer and so work out the answer to the latter.

Informal pencil and paper approaches, based on those discussed in Chapter 4, include the chunking method, which is illustrated below. Chunks of sizes 2, 20 and 12 have been used, although it is possible to carry out the calculation using chunks of other sizes.

$$
\begin{array}{r}
54 \\
0.25\,\overline{)13.5} \\
-\quad 0.5 \quad (2 \times 0.25) \\
\overline{13} \\
-\quad 5 \quad (20 \times 0.25) \\
\overline{8} \\
-\quad 5 \quad (20 \times 0.25) \\
\overline{3} \\
-\quad 3 \quad (12 \times 0.25) \\
\overline{0}
\end{array}
$$

$13.5 \div 0.25 = 54$ with no remainder

The traditional pencil and paper approach using long division, discussed in Chapter 5, is presented below. When dividing by a decimal the first stage of the procedure is to eliminate any decimal digits by multiplying both numbers by 10, 100 or 1000. In this particular example, multiplying both numbers by 100 produces the equivalent calculation $1350 \div 25$, which is then worked out using the usual division algorithm.

$$
\begin{array}{r}
5\,4 \\
2\,5\,\overline{)1\,3\,5\,0} \\
-1\,2\,5\,\downarrow \\
\overline{1\,0\,0} \\
-\,1\,0\,0 \\
\overline{0}
\end{array}
$$

It is hoped that you can now appreciate that most of the methods discussed in Chapters 3, 4 and 5 can be used with decimals as well as integers. So when faced with a calculation involving decimals, children should always consider mental methods as a first resort. If it cannot be done mentally then perhaps an informal or traditional written method provides the best alternative.

One key consideration, which was touched upon briefly in questions 1 and 2 above, is to use contexts such as money or measures as a way of avoiding decimals altogether. So, for example, when calculating $3.75 + 1.3$, think of it as money (£3.75 + £1.30) and if you do not like decimals you can simply work in pence (375p + 130p), although you will have to convert the final answer (505p) into pounds and pence by inserting the decimal point to give the final answer 5.05.

Similarly, a calculation such as 2.86×3 could be thought of in terms of three planks of wood, each 2.86 metres, laid end to end. If you do not like decimals, work in centimetres, so the calculation becomes 286cm $\times$ 3. The final answer (858cm) then needs to be converted back into metres to give 8.58. Much of the arithmetic that children carry out should have a context anyway, but if one is not provided, there is no reason why children cannot create their own in order to make the calculation more accessible.

Arithmetic with percentages

Creating percentages from a presented scenario

As was the case with fractions earlier in this chapter, some of the first percentages calculations that children have to deal with involve a scenario or visual representation from which a percentage has to be derived. Here are two typical examples.

1. What percentage of this grid is shaded?

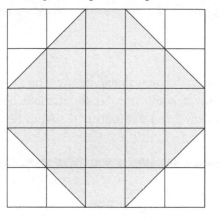

2. A child scores 18 out of 24 in a test. What is her score as a percentage?

In order to tackle these successfully children will need to understand what percentages are and how they relate to fractions other than hundredths. In the first example 17 out of 25 squares are shaded, which as a fraction is $^{17}/_{25}$. From this it is relatively straightforward to 'scale up' by a factor of 4 to create the equivalent fraction $^{68}/_{100}$ which can be written as 68%. In the second example the child's score is $^{18}/_{24}$ which cannot be scaled up to give a percentage. However, this fraction can be cancelled down to give $^{3}/_{4}$ which children should know is 75%.

Percentage parts

Percentage increases and decreases are encountered more commonly in our daily lives than are fractional parts scenarios which were discussed earlier in this chapter. It is therefore important that children are able to calculate percentage parts using everyday contexts such as those presented below for you to try.

> ### Activity
> Work out the answers to each of the following questions. You can use any method you want but must not use a calculator. Feel free to use any combination of mental methods, traditional pencil and paper methods, informal jottings and diagrams, etc. If you use a mental method, make brief notes to indicate how you actually calculated the answer.

1. Someone has £250 in a savings account, which earns 8% interest per year. How much interest is paid in the first year?
2. A restaurant meal costs £84, plus 12½% service charge. How much is the service charge?
3. A jacket costs £65 but is reduced by 15% in the sale. What is the sale price?

Before discussing sensible, efficient approaches to these problems, let's briefly look at the traditional method for tackling percentage parts questions, based on the fractions multiplication algorithm presented earlier in this chapter. The working out for the first question would be set out like this.

$$250 \times \frac{8}{100} = \frac{250}{1} \times \frac{8}{100}$$

Before multiplying the numerators and denominators, the calculation should be simplified by cancelling down. Any numerator can be cancelled with any denominator. So, for example, both 250 and 100 are divisible by 50 and so can be replaced with 5 and 2. Similarly the 8 can be cancelled with the 2.

The working out for the second question would initially look like this.

$$84 \times \frac{12\frac{1}{2}}{100} = \frac{84}{1} \times \frac{12\frac{1}{2}}{100}$$

The non-integral numerator (12½) is awkward, so this is 'scaled up' to the equivalent fraction ²⁵⁄₂₀₀ and the calculation therefore becomes:

$$= \frac{84}{1} \times \frac{25}{200}$$

As with the first example, before proceeding with the multiplication, the numerators and denominators should first be simplified by cancelling down, if this is possible.

It is not recommended that you teach these traditional algorithms because, as has been discussed on many occasions throughout this book, the danger is that children have to rely on remembering rules instead of thinking about and understanding the procedure they are using. Here are some alternative approaches for you to consider, among which you may find the ones that you used yourself.

Question 1: 8% of £250

When working out any percentage part encourage children to utilise one or two percentage parts that they are able to work out very quickly. The two obvious ones are 50% (by halving the original amount) and 10% (by dividing the original amount by 10). From one or both of these, children should be able to quickly work out virtually any other percentage part. Let's see how this principle can be utilised to work out 8% of £250.

100% of £250	= £250	
10% of £250	= £25	Divide £250 by 10.
2% of £250	= £5	Divide £25 by 5.
8% of £250	= £20	Multiply £5 by 4.

The sequence of calculations above is certainly not the only way to get to 8% of £250 and so children should be encouraged to use whatever route they wish. Also ask children to discuss and compare with one another the methods they have used.

Another approach to tackling this problem is to utilise the notion of percentage being 'parts per hundred'. So 8% means £8 in every £100. If we want 8% of £250 then that's two lots of £8 (for the £200) plus half of £8 (for the remaining £50).

Question 2: 12½% of £84

Here are two possible routes that children might take to find the answer.

100% of £84	= £84	
10% of £84	= £8.40	Divide £84 by 10.
5% of £84	= £4.20	Divide £8.40 by 2.
2½% of £84	= £2.10	Divide £4.20 by 2.
12½% of £84	= £10.50	Add 10% (£8.40) and 2½% (£2.10).

100% of £84	= £84	
50% of £84	= £42	Divide £84 by 2.
25% of £84	= £21	Divide £42 by 2.
12½% of £84	= £10.50	Divide £21 by 2.

Another possibility is that the child recognises that 12½% is ⅛ and so divides £80 by 8 (£10) and then divides £4 by 8 (50p) to produce the final answer £10.50.

Question 3: Reduce £65 by 15%

Percentage reductions such as this can be thought of in two ways. The first involves working out the 15% reduction and then subtracting this from the original amount. The second involves finding 85% of the original amount because this is what is left after a 15% reduction. These different routes to the answer are illustrated below.

100% of £65	= £65	
10% of £65	= £6.50	Divide £65 by 10.
5% of £65	= £3.25	Divide £6.50 by 2.
15% of £65	= £9.75	Add 10% and 5%.
85% of £84	= £55.25	Subtract 15% (£9.75) from 100% (£65).

100% of £65	= £65	
10% of £65	= £6.50	Divide £65 by 10.
5% of £65	= £3.25	Divide £6.50 by 2.
20% of £65	= £13	Multiply £6.50 by 2.
80% of £65	= £52	Multiply £13 by 4.
85% of £84	= £55.25	Add 80% (£52) and 5% (£3.25).

You could debate which of these two approaches (together with any others you can think of) is the most efficient, but ultimately it is a matter of preference for the individual. The key point is that we are encouraging flexible thinking instead of blind acceptance of a single set of rules. The expression 'common sense' approach has already been used in this chapter and is worth repeating again here because it aptly describes what is presented above. By way of contrast, the traditional algorithm for calculating percentage parts makes little sense to many children and adults.

Case Study: Percentages changes in stages

Anna and Craig are trainee teachers working together on some mathematics subject knowledge self-study materials provided by their tutor. They are considering ways to deal with percentage changes applied in two stages. Here is the question they are discussing.

> *A pair of shoes originally costs £60, but is reduced by 20% in the sale. A week later, in the blue cross sale, the sale prices are reduced by 25%. What is the blue cross sale price?*

Here is an extract from their discussion.

Craig: The quickest way to work it out is to add the two percentages, so that's 20% plus 25% makes 45%. Then all you do is knock 45% off the original price, although I suppose you could just work out 55% of the original price because that's what'll be left.

Anna: I don't think you can do it that way. I think you have to do it as two separate calculations – knock off 20% and then knock 25% off the sale price.

Craig: But you'll get the same answer, so you might as well do it in one go and save yourself some working out.

Activity

Study Ben and Anna's methods carefully. Without working out the answers, who do you think is correct?

Now work out the answer, first using Ben's method and then using Anna's method. You should get two different answers, but you still need to understand which one is correct!

If you use Craig's method you are reducing the original price by 20% (£12) and then by a further 25% of the original price (£15). This can be calculated as a single reduction of 45%, because both percentages are proportions of the original price. This give a total reduction of £27 and a final price of £33. However, this is not the scenario described in the question, because it states that 'the sale prices are reduced by a further 25%'. Anna's method correctly reflects this scenario because the original price is reduced by 20% (£12) to give a sale price of £48. This price is then reduced by 25% (£12) to give a final price of £36. Craig's method gives a better discount for the consumer, but it does not reflect what is described in the question.

Similar caution needs to be applied when considering a percentage increase, followed by a percentage decrease. For example, if your employer gives you a 10% pay rise and then, the following month, decides that he cannot afford it and so reduces your wages by 10%, you might be inclined to think that you would be back to your previous pay levels. However, if you work it out you will see that this is not the case, as illustrated below.

Initial wages	£500
10% increase	£50
New wages	£550
10% reduction	£55
New wages	£495

Arithmetic with ratios

Ratios, like decimals and percentages, crop up in a range of everyday contexts, as illustrated by the problems you will be attempting in this section. It is therefore important that we use real examples when teaching children what is often perceived to be a difficult aspect of mathematics.

Activity

Work out the answers to each of the following questions. You can use any method you want but must not use a calculator. Feel free to use any combination of mental methods, traditional pencil and paper methods, informal jottings and diagrams, etc. If you use a mental method, make brief notes to indicate how you actually calculated the answer.

1. A traditional TV is described as having a 4:3 screen. A modern widescreen TV is described as being 16:9. What do you think the numbers are referring to? The two screens look different when placed side by side, but how can you demonstrate arithmetically that the two screen ratios are in fact different?
2. To make marmalade you should use oranges and sugar in the ratio 5:8. If you have 3kg of oranges, how much sugar do you need?
3. The scale on a map is 1:250,000. The distance between two villages on the map is 6cm. How far apart are the villages?

> 4. Three business partners share their profits in the ratio 1:2:3. If they make £15,000 profit, how much does each partner get?

Question 1

The numbers in the ratios relate to the widths and heights of the screens. As explained at the beginning of this chapter, ratios can be 'scaled up' and 'scaled down' to create equivalent ratios. This principle can be utilised to tackle this question in two ways, as shown below.

Traditional
4 : 3
12 : 9 scale up by a factor of 3

Traditional
4 : 3
16 : 12 Scale up by a factor of 4.

The ratio 4:3 is equivalent to 12:9. Now that the second part of the ratio is the same as the second part in 16:9 it is easier to compare the two and conclude that they are different. The ratio 4:3 is also equivalent to 16:12. Again, it becomes clear that this is not the same as 16:9.

Question 2

Equivalent ratios can be used to generate possible combinations of oranges and sugar as shown below.

oranges : sugar
 5 : 8
 10 : 16
 15 : 24

These ratios are helpful if you have 5kg, 10kg, 15kg or any other multiple of 5kg of sugar, but what if you don't have a multiple of 5kg? One way of solving this is to create an equivalent ratio in which the weight of oranges is 1kg, and then multiply this by the weight of oranges you have, as shown below for 3kg oranges.

oranges : sugar
 5 : 8
 1 : $\frac{8}{5}$ Scale down by a factor of 5.
 1 : $1\frac{3}{5}$ Write the ratio as a fraction.
 1 : 1.6   Write the ratio as a decimal.
 3kg : 4.8kg   Multiply by 3 (or 'scale up' by a factor of 3).

Sometimes we prefer to write ratios using only integers, for example the ratio 5 : 8, whereas on other occasions, particularly when carrying calculations like the one above, it is preferable to have the ratio in the form 1 : n, even if n is not an integer.

Question 3

Here is one possible way of tackling this problem.

```
map  :  land
  1  :  250,000
1cm  :  250,000cm
1cm  :  2,500m
1cm  :  2.5km
6cm  :  15km
```

Question 4

The distinction between ratio and proportion was discussed briefly earlier in this chapter in relation to mixing concrete and that distinction will be employed here. If profits are shared in the ratio 1:2:3 then this means that the first person gets $\frac{1}{6}$ of the profits, the second gets $\frac{2}{6}$ (which is $\frac{1}{3}$) and the third gets $\frac{3}{6}$ (which is $\frac{1}{2}$); $\frac{1}{6}$ of £15,000 is £2500, $\frac{1}{3}$ is £5000 and $\frac{1}{2}$ is £7500.

Implications for your teaching

The first important implication is that before introducing children to arithmetic involving fractions, decimals, percentages and ratios, you must first ensure that they have the necessary understanding of these concepts. It is possible for children to follow a set of memorised rules to multiply two fractions or to calculate a percentage part, but with no conceptual understanding of what fractions and percentages actually represent. Is this really the sort of learning you want to promote and your children to experience? Instead this arithmetic should be tackled using a 'common sense' approach, but this is only possible if children possess a thorough understanding of the prerequisites discussed earlier.

The second implication is that all of the arithmetical processes considered in the preceding chapters should be taught and encouraged if we want children to calculate efficiently with fractions, decimals, percentages and ratios. These aspects of mathematics are associated with the upper primary years and so it is tempting to think only in terms of traditional pencil and paper approaches. However, instant recall, flexible mental methods and informal written approaches are all as applicable to non-integers as they are to integers, and so represent an essential element of the progression in your teaching and in children's learning.

Learning Outcomes Review

You should now understand what children in primary schools need to be taught in relation to fractions, decimals, percentages and ratios. This understanding relates to laying the necessary foundations for children's arithmetic, and also to the arithmetical processes themselves in terms of what should realistically be expected of children. Additionally, you should now possess the subject knowledge to enable you to calculate effectively using fractions, decimals, percentages and

---

ratios, utilising approaches based on instant recall, mental methods and a variety of written methods. You should also have the pedagogical understanding to equip you to teach these aspects of number appropriately and effectively, including the identification of some of the errors and misconceptions that children commonly make.

Self-assessment questions

1. Tom and Sally each start with the same amount of money. Tom spends two-thirds of his. Sally spends five-sixths of hers. In total they have £12 left. How much did they each have at the start?

2. Use an efficient method to calculate
   a. $9.8 - 7.75$
   b. 20×3.875

3. A coat is reduced by 20% in the sale. The sale price is £60. What was the original price?

4. A model aircraft is made using the scale 1:72.
   a. the propeller of the model has a diameter of 2.5cm. What is the diameter of the real propeller?
   b. the wingspan of the real aircraft is 20 metres. What is the wingspan of the model? (You can use a calculator for this part of the question.)

Further Reading

DfE (2010) *Teaching children to calculate mentally.* London: DfE Publications. There is a short section on fractions, decimals and percentages towards the end of this publication (pages 69–71).

Hansen, A. (ed.) (2011) *Children's Errors in Mathematics* (2nd Edition). London: Learning Matters. In particular have a look at the fractions, decimals, percentages and ratio and proportion sections of Chapters 3 and 4.

Mooney, C., Ferrie, L., Fox, S., Hansen, A. and Wrathmell, R. (2011) *Primary Mathematics: Knowledge and Understanding.* London: Learning Matters. There are several sections of Chapter 2 ('Number') that provide a good introduction to fractions, decimals, percentages and ratios.

QCA (1999) *Teaching Written Calculations: Guidance for teachers at Key Stages 1 and 2.* Sudbury: QCA Publications. Part 5 considers fractions, decimals and percentages.

References

DfE (2012) *National Curriculum for Mathematics: Key Stages 1 and 2 – Draft.* London: DfE Publications.

Hart, K.M. (ed.) (1981) *Children's Understanding of Mathematics: 11–16*. London: John Murray Ltd.

Kieren, T.E. (1976) On the Mathematical, Cognitive, and Instructional Foundations of Rational Numbers, in Lesh, R.A. and Brandberd, D.A. (eds) *Number and Measurement*. Columbus, Ohio: ERIC/SMEAC.

Mooney, C., Ferrie, L., Fox, S., Hansen, A. and Wrathmell, R. (2012) *Primary Mathematics: Knowledge and Understanding*. London: Learning Matters.

7. Arithmetic using technology

Learning Outcomes
....

By the end of this chapter you will:
- have an appreciation of the historical perspective and associated research, evaluation and inspection evidence relating to the role of technology, with a particular focus on calculators;
- be aware of the curriculum requirements with regard to the use of technology;
- understand key technical and pedagogical issues associated with utilising calculators and spreadsheets to support arithmetic in the primary school.

Introduction

Technology is an ever-present feature of our everyday lives, including on those occasions when we carry out arithmetic, and so it is wholly appropriate that this book should consider its utilisation. There are very few adults who do not have easy access to tools such as calculators, mobile phones, tablets, netbooks, laptops and desktop computers, all of which have the facility to carry out calculations. It is therefore vitally important that we equip children to make use of these devices effectively and this process must begin in the primary school. However, the use of technology polarises opinions and generates more conflict than perhaps any other aspect of teaching mathematics. Technology is universally recognised as being of intrinsic value, but at the same time certain aspects of it, for example calculators, are sometimes afforded demonic status and held up as the reason for children's lack of numeracy skills. One of the aims of this chapter is to dispel some of the myths surrounding the use of technology in the primary school by considering the research and inspection evidence that has emerged in recent years. Additionally, a number of issues relating to the use of technology to support arithmetic teaching will be explored. This chapter is not intended to provide a general discussion of the utilisation of technology in mathematics. Instead, the focus will be very much on arithmetic and so this will, in effect, be in relation to calculators and spreadsheets because these are the two most common calculating tools available in primary schools.

Historical background

Before considering the current and likely future curriculum expectations in relation to arithmetic and technology, the historical perspective will be discussed. This will help to clarify some of the unwarranted headlines and misinformation that have been circulated over the years.

The first affordable hand-held calculators started to become popular in the mid 1970s and it was shortly after this that an HMI, Michael Girling (1977, page 4), proposed that *Basic numeracy is the ability to use a four-function calculator sensibly*. He went on to conclude that the teaching objectives in relation to pencil and paper arithmetic in the primary school would therefore need to be re-examined. These views were shared by Plunkett who stated that:

> The advent of calculators has provided us with a great opportunity. We are freed from the necessity to provide every citizen with methods for dealing with calculations of indefinite complexity. So we can abandon the standard written algorithms, of general applicability and limited intelligibility, in favour of methods more suited to the minds and purposes of the users. With mental methods occupying their proper place as the principal means for doing simple calculations, the position of calculators is clear. They are the sensible tool for difficult calculations, the ideal complement to mental arithmetic.

> *(1979, page 5)*

The Cockcroft Report (DES, 1982) afforded a whole chapter to calculators and computers, presenting a very positive view of their potential impact, but at the same time stating that:

> it remains incumbent upon those who teach mathematics to ensure that the development of appropriate skills of written and mental calculation is not neglected.

> *(page 110)*

It was also noted that the research evidence available at that time indicated that the use of calculators did not produce any adverse effects on children's arithmetical competence.

Between 1985 and 1989 a government-funded primary curriculum development project was instigated, including one component which advocated a 'Calculator-Aware Number' (CAN) curriculum. The impact of this was very positive and the findings could therefore not be ignored by those responsible for writing the forthcoming National Curriculum (DES, 1989a). Consequently the new curriculum contained several references to the use of calculators. For example the children working at level 2 were expected to check additions and subtractions with a calculator, and those working at level 3 to solve multiplication and division problems involving whole numbers, using a calculator where necessary. At levels 3 and 4 children were expected to be able to interpret calculator displays appropriately, for example in relation to rounding and in the context of money problems. However, the most significant acknowledgement of calculators in the 1989 mathematics National Curriculum appeared in the non-statutory guidance, which included a section on 'Calculator Methods', stating that they:

> provide a powerful and versatile tool for pupils to use in both the development of their understanding of number and for doing calculations

> *(DES, 1989b, page E5).*

The guidance also suggested that calculators should be made available to children across all key stages. By way of summary, the guidance advocated a balanced approach in which the introduction of calculators would result in mental methods assuming greater importance, while the heavy emphasis on traditional written methods would require careful re-examination.

On the face of it the National Curriculum appeared to be promoting a very positive stance on the use of calculators, although it is worth noting that within the programmes of study the phrase *without a calculator* occurred more frequently than those encouraging calculator use, leading to one commentator to observe that:

> *Beneath the veneer of calculator recognition, both the national curriculum and national testing emerged as more 'calculator-beware' in spirit than 'calculator-aware'.*

> (Ruthven, 2001, page 171)

Despite the increased emphasis on the use of calculators in the National Curriculum, inspection evidence noted that in *very few of the lessons in either Key Stage 1 or Key Stage 2 was use made of calculators to enhance the experience and performance of pupils* (Ofsted, 1993a, page 13) and *the skills of using a calculator were neglected in a high percentage of schools* (Ofsted 1993b, page 11). These low levels of calculator use were also reported in a government discussion paper, which reviewed much of the available research and inspection evidence and concluded that with regard to the primary phase:

> *The degree of calculator use remains modest in most schools and by most pupils. Given the patterns of use currently typical of schools, the influence of the calculator on attainment and attitudes is relatively unimportant. However tempting it may be to cast the calculator as scapegoat for disappointing mathematical performance at primary level, the available evidence provides scant support for this position, which may serve only to distract attention from more influential factors.*

> (SCAA, 1997, page 18)

Presumably the *more influential factors* are things such as the lack of emphasis on mental methods and the recall of number facts, the over-emphasis on traditional pencil and paper methods, the tendency to teach traditional pencil and paper methods far too early, and the overuse of individualised commercial schemes and consequent absence of any whole-class teaching. All of these were common deficiencies reported by Ofsted during the years leading up to the introduction of the National Numeracy Strategy.

The government's launch of the National Numeracy Strategy in 1998 was accompanied by news reports and headlines announcing the 'banning' of calculators from primary schools. In reality the final report of the Numeracy Task Force recommended nothing of the sort, instead stating that:

> *There is no place for using calculators as a prop for simple arithmetic, since children are still learning the mental calculation skills and written methods that they will need throughout their lives. Used well, however, calculators can be an effective tool for learning about numbers and the number system, such as place value, precision, and fractions and decimals.*

> (DfEE, 1998, page 52)

Despite all the in-service training and associated support documentation provided by the National Numeracy Strategy and the Primary National Strategy over the last 12 years, there still appears to be much confusion and uncertainty among primary teachers regarding how they should be utilising calculators. This is reflected in the inspection findings of Ofsted which report that:

Teachers remain uncertain about when and how often to use calculators as part of their daily mathematics lessons.

(Ofsted, 2000, page 18)

and:

There is not enough good use of calculators, either as a teaching tool or by the pupils themselves, in the daily mathematics lesson at Key Stage 2.

(Ofsted, 2002, page 4)

It would appear that this limited use of technology is persisting, with Ofsted reporting that:

Most of the schools visited introduce calculators in upper Key Stage 2, principally for the purpose of checking by pupils of their answers to calculations.

(Ofsted, 2011, page 28)

and:

Several of the schools acknowledged that they could make better use of calculators and information and communication technology in mathematics, an issue not restricted to this sample of schools.

(Ofsted, 2011, page 29)

This historical perspective, based on research, government publications and inspection evidence, would suggest that the potential offered by calculators and spreadsheets, identified by Cockcroft over thirty years ago, is still not being realised. It is hoped that the remainder of this chapter will make some contribution to addressing this, although government policy and new National Curriculum requirements will play a crucial role.

Research Focus: The CAN Project

The CAN project was a curriculum development initiative extending over four years from 1986 to 1989. This initially involved 20 primary schools, identified in small clusters throughout England and Wales, although over time an increasing number of other schools adopted the principles advocated by the project. These principles included:

* a strong emphasis on mathematical understanding through the use of practical, investigative, problem-solving activities and the development of mathematical language;

→

- the promotion of mental methods, with the traditional pencil and paper methods not being taught unless individual teachers wanted to – in most cases if a calculation could not be carried out mentally, children used a calculator;

- open access to calculators at all times, with decisions about calculator use being taken by the children, not their teachers.

The project report (Shuard et al., 1991) indicates that children's learning did not progress in the linear way that many teachers typically expected. Instead, children were given the freedom to take responsibility for their own learning and so constructed their own networks of mathematical concepts. Systematic evaluation of attainment was not part of the project, although anecdotal evidence reported very positive outcomes for both the children and their teachers. However, research outcomes relating to the impact of the CAN project have been reported by other authors.

Oram (1989) analysed the test results of 116 children in Suffolk's four CAN project schools and compared these with the results of 116 children randomly selected from non-CAN schools. The children from the CAN schools performed better in 26 out of 36 questions, the non-CAN children scored better in six questions and in the remaining four questions there was no difference. However, Oram also reports that the margin of difference was far greater in the 26 questions where the CAN children were outperforming their peers than in the six questions where the reverse was true.

An evaluation by Rowland (1994) notes that 6- and 7-year-olds in CAN schools were comfortable with large numbers and developed efficient mental methods for working with numbers up to 100. He also reports a positive impact on teachers, with many increasing their expectations of children's mathematical capabilities as a result of being involved in the project.

Ruthven (2001) summarises the research carried out by his team in the late 1990s in which former CAN project schools were compared with schools that had not been involved with the project at all. In terms of the curriculum at Key Stage 1 Ruthven found that non-CAN schools were very much wedded to the teaching of traditional arithmetic written in columns, with very limited use of calculators. In contrast, the former CAN schools viewed arithmetic as something that should emerge through investigation and problem solving, supported by mental methods and the frequent use of calculators. However, in Key Stage 2 Ruthven found a gradual convergence of these two broad approaches, with the non-CAN schools starting to take account of the National Curriculum requirements relating to problem solving, mental arithmetic and the use of calculators. Ruthven's research also examined the results of national testing at ages 7 and 11. At the end of Key Stage 1 there was no overall difference between the former CAN and non-CAN schools, although the former CAN schools had more children at the extremes of the

$\rightarrow$

attainment scale, that is, achieving levels 1 and 3. This situation was not mirrored at the end of Key Stage 2, but it was observed that children from former CAN schools were more likely to use mental methods when calculating and were capable of developing a range of powerful and efficient strategies.

What children need to know – curriculum requirements

The curriculum requirements of the 1999 National Curriculum make no explicit reference to technology in the Key Stage 1 programme of study. However, at Key Stage 2, children should be taught to:

> *Find percentages of whole number quantities, using a calculator where appropriate. Use a calculator for calculations involving several digits, including decimals; use a calculator to solve number problems; know how to enter and interpret money calculations and fractions; know how to select the correct key sequence for calculations with more than one operation.*

> *(DfEE/QCA, 1999, pages 68–70)*

At the time of writing this book the primary curriculum is under review, although as part of this process the Expert Panel for the National Curriculum review has recommended that:

> *Information and communication technology is reclassified as part of the Basic Curriculum and requirements should be established so that it permeates all National Curriculum subjects.*

> *(DfE, 2011, page 24)*

Of more specific relevance to mathematics, government minister Nick Gibb (DfE, 2011) has stated that *the use of calculators in primary schools would be looked at as part of the National Curriculum Review*. These announcements have been followed more recently by the publication of draft programmes of study for primary mathematics (DfE, 2012). The introduction includes a section on the use of information and communication technology and states that calculators *should not be used as a substitute for pupils having poor written and mental arithmetic* and *should therefore only be introduced near the end of primary* (DfE, 2012, page 2). The document also states the value of other technological tools such as spreadsheets, graphing programs and simulation software. However, in the programmes of study themselves, there is no mention of technology at all apart from stating that a calculator could be used in Year 6 to convert fractions into decimals.

Given this backdrop, it will be interesting to see how the curricular requirements and related non-statutory guidance relating to the use of technology in primary mathematics evolve over the next few years.

What children need to know – using the technology

Assuming technology continues to have a role in supporting children's arithmetic, it is important that teachers understand what children need to be taught in order to use the technology effectively. The evidence presented in the previous sections would suggest that many primary teachers are currently not equipping children to make the most of the available technology. It is therefore proposed that teachers address the following five areas in their teaching.

Knowing when it is appropriate to use the technology

Children need to have the knowledge and understanding to make appropriate choices with regard to the use of calculators, spreadsheets and technology in general. We do not want children to be using calculators for arithmetic that should be done mentally or using written methods, but at the same time we should not be expecting children to be carrying out complex arithmetic without access to a calculator. Some children will develop the ability to make sensible choices themselves, but many will require clear guidance from the teacher. So, as part of your teaching, you need to discuss with children the options that are available in terms of mental, written and calculator approaches when faced with a particular calculation.

The technical aspects of using the technology

It sounds blindingly obvious, but children need to know what to do with the technology in order to use it effectively, and this implies that the teacher must have the necessary technical knowledge to teach the children. In the case of calculators it would be tempting to nonchalantly suggest that everyone knows which buttons to press in order to get an answer, but there's more to the humble four-function calculator than most teachers think. When was the last time you used the memory facility on a calculator? Be honest! Most people never use it. Why? Because they've never been shown how to and so instead they have to rely on scribbled intermediate answers on scraps of paper. Similarly with a spreadsheet, it is likely that many teachers do not have the technical knowledge to use one effectively, either for their own professional use, or as part of their teaching. All of these sorts of technical aspects will be considered later in this chapter.

Understanding what needs to be calculated

Teachers frequently report that children are not very good at 'word problems', which require them to decipher information and decide which calculations need to be carried out. These sorts of situations may or may not involve children using calculators and are part of the wider issue of children not being very good at problem solving, although please note that 'word problems' represent only a very limited subset of what constitutes meaningful problem solving in mathematics. This inability to 'spot the operation' is not restricted to children, as you may discover when you attempt the following activity.

You probably know how to work out means (add up the marks and divide by how many marks there are) and how to use a calculator to add, subtract, multiply and divide. However, this activity may have presented a challenge for you because it requires you to utilise your understanding of how to calculate means in an unfamiliar way. If your range of experiences in using means is limited to routine situations, then you probably found this question difficult to decipher. The same is true for children. We cannot expect them to be able to make appropriate decisions about which calculation to carry out if we do not provide them with opportunities to develop the necessary problem-solving skills.

Just in case you need it, here is a solution to the question.

Total marks for all children	$= 32 \times 42.81$	$= 1370$
Total marks for 19 girls	$= 19 \times 46.21$	$= 878$
Total marks for 13 boys	$= 1370 - 878$	$= 492$
Mean mark for 13 boys	$= 492 \div 13$	$= 37.85\%$

Interpreting the results produced by the technology

In the solution presented above the results displayed by the calculator needed to be interpreted and dealt with appropriately. So, for example, 32×42.81 gives the answer 1369.92, but given that this represents the total number of marks obtained by the 32 children, this needs to be adjusted to 1370. This is because when originally calculating the mean mark, 1370 was divided by 32 to produce a decimal answer, which was recorded as 42.81 when rounded to two decimal places. This is just one example of how the results presented by technological tools need to be interpreted appropriately. One of the earliest examples that children encounter is when the calculator does not always display two digits after the decimal point when dealing with money problems and so £4.60 is displayed as 4.6. Other examples, relating to both calculators and spreadsheets, will be considered later in the chapter.

The importance of estimation and approximation

Whenever children carry out any calculation, be it mentally or using written methods, they should always have a rough idea of what the answer should be so that they can assess the reasonableness of their solution. This is crucially important when using technological tools because it is so tempting to blindly accept the answers that are produced. Children need to appreciate that technology is not infallible because human error can result in the wrong button being pressed or the wrong formula being typed. The relevant estimation skills, which in turn are dependent upon the ability to approximate, therefore need to feature strongly in your teaching long before children start to use technology. Then, once children start to utilise calculators and computers you must always encourage them to estimate so that they are constantly asking themselves the question 'Does the answer look reasonable?'

Arithmetic with a calculator

The aim of this section is to provide you with the necessary knowledge and skills to utilise all of the facilities offered by a typical calculator found in primary schools. Issues relating to the interpretation of the displayed results and decisions about the final answer to a problem will also be considered.

The C, AC and CE keys

Depending on the particular calculator you are using it is likely to have one or more of the following keys: C (clear); CE (clear entry); CA or AC (clear all). Some calculators have only a C key which can be pressed once (clear entry) or pressed twice to clear the complete calculation (clear all). These keys are useful if, when adding a lengthy list of numbers, you enter one of them incorrectly. If you press the 'clear all' key you have to start again from scratch. However, pressing the 'clear entry' key results in only the last entry being cleared, enabling you to enter the correct number and continue with the calculation. By using this facility you can save yourself (and your children) a lot of wasted time!

The constant function

Press the following keys on your calculator and watch the display.

The constant function can be used in this way to count on in any step, either whole numbers or decimals.

It can be used to count back in any step and from any starting number, for example:

Multiplication and division can be used to carry out repeated doubling and halving, for example:

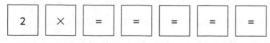

(Please note that these key presses may not work with all calculators and so slight variations may be required.)

Precedence of operations

This important issue is best demonstrated by the following case study.

> ### Case Study: Precedence of operations when using calculators
>
> Maggie wants to introduce the use of brackets to her Year 5 class. She writes the following on the board and asks the children to work out the answer.
>
> $2 \times 3 + 4 \times 5 =$
>
> All of the children agree that the answer is 50, although Maggie was hoping that one of them might suggest 26. She hands a calculator to one of the children and asks her to type in the number sentence, just as it has been written on the board. The calculator also gives the answer 50. Then Maggie gives a different calculator to another child and asks him to type in the same number sentence. Here is an extract from the dialogue that follows.
>
> **Maggie:** So, James, what did you get?
>
> **James:** 26, Miss.
>
> **Maggie:** That's interesting! So we've got two calculators giving us different answers. Jemma's calculator gave us 50, you all said the answer is 50, but James's calculator is giving us 26. Can anyone work out how James's calculator is getting that answer?
>
> After a short period of thinking time one of the children correctly explains that the second calculator has done the two multiplications first and then added the answers. Because the main focus for this lesson is the use of brackets to indicate precedence, Maggie goes on to discuss with the children how they might indicate in a number sentence that a particular calculation should be done first. One child suggests putting a ring around each of the multiplications, another child suggests a box around each, but they eventually decide that brackets would be an ideal solution.

The key message in relation to calculators is to ensure that you (and the children) know the precedence that your calculators give to the various operations because, as illustrated in the case study above, calculators operate in different ways.

Displaying large numbers

Use a calculator to work out the following and see what you get in the display.

$235,000 \times 14,000$

You may get an error message because the calculator simply cannot display such a large answer. Alternatively the calculator might display

3.29   09   or   3.29   E09

This is an abbreviated version of standard form or scientific notation. The E stands for 'exponent' and so the 09 part of the answer is a power of 10. The number displayed is therefore

3.29×10^9

which can be written as

$3.29 \times 1,000,000,000$

which is

3,290,000,000

This level of mathematics is beyond the expectations of children in primary schools, but it is important that you know how to interpret results such as this. Able pupils in upper Key Stage 2 might stumble upon this notation by accident and ask you to explain it to them, so be prepared! The other issue you might like to consider is how to calculate $145,000 \times 18,000$ without a calculator, making use of your knowledge of equivalence and the associative law, discussed in Chapter 3.

The memory facility

The memory facility can be found on most simple calculators used in primary schools, but, as discussed earlier in this chapter, it is very much underused.

The memory facility usually comprises four keys which are described below.

M+   Press this key and whatever is in the display is added to the memory.
M−   Press this key and whatever is in the display is subtracted from the memory.
MR   Press this key to display the number stored in the memory.
CM   Press this key to clear the memory.

By using the memory you can save yourself the trouble of jotting down intermediate answers when tackling a problem as demonstrated in the case study below.

Case Study: The effective use of the memory facility

Tom wants his Year 6 children to use their understanding of the relationships between the four operations, together with their trial and improvement skills and calculator proficiency, to tackle some 'Broken Keys' questions. Here is one of the questions Tom presents to the children.

$\rightarrow$

The multiplication key is broken. Work out 15.29 × 4.75 using your calculator.

Many of the children are able to work out the answer using the inverse relationship between multiplication and division, together with trial and improvement, as illustrated below.

Answer =   15.29 × 4.75

Therefore ...

Answer ÷ 4.75 = 15.29

One child's first estimate for the answer is 75:   75 ÷ 4.75 = 15.789

So he adjusts this and then tries 74:   74 ÷ 4.75 = 15.579

He continues this process to eventually find the correct answer.

During the plenary Tom models another way of tackling this problem, without using the multiplication key, but making use of the memory facility. Here are the key presses he uses.

Four lots of 15.29 are added to the memory.

The calculator now displays one quarter of 15.29.

Three-quarters of 15.29 is added to the memory, so that is 4.75 lots stored in the memory altogether.

Finally, he presses the MR button to recall the memory and display the answer.

This approach provides Tom with an excellent opportunity to discuss the memory facility, as well as other important aspects of number, for example the distributive law (i.e. 4.75 lots is equivalent to 4 lots plus 0.75 lots) and the relationship between fractions and decimals (i.e. 0.75 is ¾).

Knowing the answer to the question

In the section on 'Displaying large numbers' above, the matter of interpreting the calculator display was considered, but this very specific notation issue needs to be broadened to include other difficulties that children encounter when using calculators to establish the final answer to a problem. Here are some examples of the sorts of things you will need to address in your teaching if you want children to use calculators effectively.

- Understanding the notion of recurring decimals and knowing that these can often be expressed as a fraction.

- Rounding decimal answers so that they are given to an appropriate level of accuracy, for example to one, two or three decimal places or to the nearest whole number.

- Rounding answers to money problems appropriately to the nearest penny or pound. This also applies to problems involving other units of measure such as metres, centimetres, litres, millilitres and so on.

- Rounding up appropriately, even if the numerical result should be rounded down. For example, if 12,000 items are to be despatched in boxes of 144, then 84 boxes will be needed even though $12,000 \div 144 = 83.33$ which would normally be rounded down.

- Rounding down appropriately, even if the numerical result should be rounded up. For example, if a school has collected 27,483 computer vouchers and 5750 vouchers can be exchanged for one computer, only four computers can be claimed, even though $27,483 \div 5750 = 4.78$ which would normally be rounded up.

Arithmetic with a spreadsheet

In the limited space available here it is not possible to provide a comprehensive set of training materials to equip you to use all of the facilities offered by a spreadsheet. However, a few basic technical aspects will be considered to enable you to start to employ a spreadsheet as an arithmetical tool with your children. One important thing to be aware of is the fact that there are a number of different spreadsheets available and so the precise syntax used in formulae and built-in functions may vary from one product to another, although it is believed that the aspects presented here are employed fairly consistently across all spreadsheets.

What is a spreadsheet?

A spreadsheet can be thought of as a table or grid, comprising many cells, which are arranged in columns and rows. The columns are labelled using letters (A, B, C, etc.) and the rows are labelled using numbers (1, 2, 3, etc.). This allows each cell to be identified using a cell reference such as B7, rather like the way that squares can be identified on a 'street-map' style co-ordinates grid, which children first encounter in Key Stage 1. However, please note that whereas a typical co-ordinates grid has square A1 in the bottom left corner, cell A1 on a spreadsheet is in the top-left corner.

Into the cells it is possible to type two sorts of information.

- Data: these can be numbers, text (for example as labels or column headings) or dates. To do this you simply click on a cell and start typing.

- A formula: this usually refers to other cells on the spreadsheet and can include various arithmetical operations or built-in functions. A formula must begin with an equals sign, otherwise the spreadsheet does not recognise it as a formula and treats it as a piece of text. Again, all you have to do is click on a cell and start typing the formula, but when it has been entered, it is the result of the formula which is displayed, not the formula itself.

It is the formulae and built-in functions which make a spreadsheet such a powerful mathematical tool, because even based on just the four standard arithmetical operations it is possible to create complex models and simulations, as well as carry out routine calculations efficiently.

Simple formulae

Here are some examples of formulae that can be typed into cells on a spreadsheet. It is assumed that cells A1, A2 and A3 already contain numbers, which could be whole numbers or decimals. If you are not already familiar with spreadsheets you might like to try this yourself. Start by typing any three different numbers into cells A1, A2 and A3. Type the formulae presented below into cells C1, C2, C3, etc. (one formula in each cell).

=A1+A2+A3	The sum will be displayed in C1.
=A1-A2	The difference will be displayed in C2.
=A1*A2	The product will be displayed in C3 (note that an asterisk is used to denote multiplication).
–A1/A2	The quotient will be displayed (note that the 'slash' is used to denote division).
=A1*(A2+A3)	Note that multiple operations can be used, possibly with brackets to indicate precedence.

If you change any of the numbers in A1, A2 or A3, the results in column C will be updated automatically to take account of the new values. Try it for yourself!

Built-in functions

Suppose you have a list of children's test scores in cells A1 to A30. You might want to display the total of these scores in cell A32. You could do this by typing the following formula.

=A1+A2+A3+A4 ... (You would have to type all of the cell references!)

There is a quicker alternative to this, as shown below.

=SUM(A1:A30)

Similarly you can display the mean score in cell A33 by typing the following.

=AVERAGE(A1:A30)

Important presentation issues

It is possible to create visually stunning effects by experimenting with font types, font sizes, borders, shadings and so on, but it is beyond the scope of this book to consider them here. However, two important issues relating to the way that numbers are displayed will be discussed.

The first relates to the way that numbers representing money appear in the cells. As discussed earlier in the chapter, a calculator does not know that you are dealing with money and so £4.50 will be displayed as 4.5. The same is true of a spreadsheet and so, by default, the same will happen. However, all spreadsheets offer the facility to have a certain number of decimal places fixed, so that they are always displayed, even if some or all of the trailing digits are zeros. So in the case of money you could have two fixed decimal places, or in the case of kilograms and grams you could have three fixed decimal places.

The second issue relates to the way that spreadsheets deal with very large numbers. Again, this has been discussed earlier in relation to calculators, where the concept of standard form using exponents was introduced. Spreadsheets operate in a similar fashion and so if a cell is not sufficiently wide to display a number in its entirety, it might be displayed as shown in cell C6 below.

	A	B	C
1	Number	Doubled	Squared
2	1	2	1
3	2	4	4
4	3	6	9
5	4	8	16
6	93500	187000	8.74E+09

Columns B and C contain formulae which double and square the numbers in column A. The number in C6 has been displayed using an exponent and so, in standard form would be written

$$8.74 \times 10^9$$

which is

8,740,000,000

Also note that on the spreadsheet, due to the lack of space, the number has been rounded to three significant figures, because the exact answer is in fact 8,742,250,000. You can usually avoid this notation and the rounding of answers by simply making the columns wider, but it is important that you and your children understand what to do when presented with this sort of notation on a spreadsheet.

Ways of using a spreadsheet

It is not possible here to provide comprehensive coverage of the ways that spreadsheets can be utilised in primary mathematics and so possible sources of additional information are provided at the end of the chapter. However, by way of summary, here are a few brief suggestions for you to investigate further.

- Record data on a spreadsheet and then use formulae and built-in functions to calculate totals, means, percentages and so on. Most spreadsheets also have powerful graphing facilities.

- Use a spreadsheet to generate and explore number sequences, such as square numbers, cubed numbers, triangular numbers, the Fibonacci sequence and so on. Investigate the ratios between consecutive numbers in these sorts of sequences by using division.

- Investigate the effects of repeated halving, or repeated division by 3. What happens when all the calculated answers are added together?

- Model real situations involving money using a spreadsheet, for example the cost of a class party, savings returns using various interest rates, the cost of items after different percentage discounts, the effects of different VAT rates and so on.

- Model scenarios involving other measures such as length, area, weight and capacity, for example investigate the areas of different rectangles that all have a fixed perimeter.

- Use various formulae to produce 'function machines' or 'input-output' machines. These could be simple one-step machines or multi-step.

- Try to produce a 100-square, or multiplication tables square, as well as other number grids, but without typing all of the numbers. Instead, you have to make use of formulae which can be copied across rows and down columns to produce the numbers in the grid.

- Use the random number generating facility (all spreadsheets have this) to simulate the flicking of coins or rolling of dice. Then use the spreadsheet to calculate average scores and to graph the outcomes.

Case Study: Using a spreadsheet to model a practical activity

As part of the shape and measures work with her Year 6 class Gabby presents the children with a practical investigative activity. Working with the whole class, Gabby starts with a piece of squared paper, measuring 20cm by 20cm. Then she cuts a single square out of each corner and folds up the edges of the paper to make a shallow box. The children have to work out how many centi-cubes (1cm by 1cm by 1cm) can be fitted into the box. Gabby discusses the answer with the children ($18 \times 18 = 324$) and also asks them to explain how they worked it out. Then she cuts a 2cm by 2cm square out of each corner and again folds up the edges of the paper to make another box. She asks the children to discuss in pairs how many

$\rightarrow$

centi-cubes would fit in this box ($16 \times 16 \times 2 = 512$) and then extends this to a whole-class discussion. The children then work in pairs, investigating the maximum number of centi-cubes that can be fitted into these sorts of boxes, formed by cutting increasingly bigger squares from the corners of a 20cm by 20cm piece of paper. Some children choose to do this as a practical activity, while others are able to visualise the boxes without actually making them.

When they have found the maximum, the extension task is to investigate whether an even bigger box can be made if the dimensions of the cut-outs in the corners are no longer restricted to being whole numbers of centimetres. For example, if the children now want to cut out a 2.7cm by 2.7cm square from each corner, they can. The resulting box is 14.6cm long, 14.6cm wide, 2.7cm tall, and has a volume of 575.532cm^3. For this stage of the activity the children are allowed to use calculators, whereas earlier, when using whole numbers, Gabby asked them to use mental and written methods.

During the plenary Gabby discusses the children's results and methods. Finally, she demonstrates how this activity can be modelled on a spreadsheet. The children already know how to use simple formulae on a spreadsheet so are able to assist Gabby in producing what is shown below.

	A	B	C	D	E	F
1	Cut-out	Length	Width	Height	Volume	
2	1	18	18	1	324	
3	2	16	16	2	512	
4	3	14	14	3	588	
5	4	12	12	4	576	
6	5	10	10	5	500	
7	6	8	8	6	384	
8	3.5	13	13	3.5	591.5	
9	3.4	13.2	13.2	3.4	592.416	
10	3.3	13.4	13.4	3.3	592.548	
11	3.35	13.3	13.3	3.35	592.5815	
12						

The cells in columns B to E contain formulae and so the only numbers that are actually typed in are those in column A; everything else is calculated automatically by the spreadsheet. The formulae are initially typed into row 2 and then copied into the rows below. This spreadsheet enables Gabby to further develop the children's trial and improvement skills during the plenary and they are quickly able to spot patterns in the results and make predictions. They conclude that the maximum volume is obtained using a cut-out with dimensions 3.333 (recurring). Of

$\longrightarrow$

course, being an investigative activity, there is always a further extension and so Gabby leaves the children to ponder on whether it would have been the same conclusion if they had started with a 15cm by 15cm square!

Activity

Can you work out the formulae that Gabby typed into cells B2, C2, D2 and E2? If you can, then perhaps you would like to create the spreadsheet and try the investigation for yourself.

Here is an explanation, just in case you were not able to work out the necessary formulae.

Cell B2 displays the length of the box, which is 20, less two lots of the cut-out dimension (which is already in cell A2). The formula is therefore

=20−2*A2

Cell C2 displays the width of the box, which is exactly the same as the length. The simplest formula is therefore

=B2

Cell D2 displays the height of the box, which is equivalent to the size of the cut-out dimension in cell A2, so the formula is

=A2

Cell E2 displays the volume of the box, which is the product of the length, width and height. The formula is therefore

=B2*C2*D2

As well as getting you to think about the technicalities of using a spreadsheet and providing you with an activity to try with your children, it is hoped that this case study also highlights the fact that by utilising technology to perform routine low-level calculations, the children were able to focus their attention on higher-level skills such as problem solving, reasoning and the identification of patterns and relationships.

Implications for your teaching

Technological issues

If you want to use technology effectively in your teaching, with the ultimate aim of enhancing children's learning, your first priority is to ensure that you have the relevant technical knowledge. This includes things such as understanding how to use the memory facility on a calculator and knowing the specific syntax issues for the formulae and functions of the spreadsheet that is available in your school. Unless you possess this technical knowledge and understanding you cannot possibly start to integrate technology into your mathematics teaching.

Pedagogical issues

Utilising technology in your teaching is not simply a case of giving children access to it and providing them with technical instructions. You must also ensure that the relevant pedagogical issues are considered, for example by laying the necessary foundations of children's estimation skills and teaching children how to interpret the results produced by the technology. There is also the wider issue of ensuring that children's experiences of using calculators and spreadsheets extend beyond the execution of routine calculations to include problem solving and investigative work. This in turn requires an ability to interpret a solution in the context of the problem or scenario that has been presented, rather than simply quoting what appears in the calculator display or in the cells of the spreadsheet. If you address these pedagogical considerations your children will be able to fully exploit the technology by letting it take care of the low-level mechanical tasks, thus freeing up time which can be spent on higher-level skills such as analysis, interpretation and hypothesising.

Appropriate use of technology

Linked to the broad pedagogical considerations mentioned above is the crucial issue of ensuring that the technology is used appropriately, particularly with regard to children's decisions about which arithmetical approach to adopt. We certainly do not want children using calculators for arithmetic that can be carried out mentally, but at the other extreme we do not want children using pencil and paper arithmetic when it is sensible to use a calculator or spreadsheet, as demonstrated in the case study above ('Using a spreadsheet to model a practical activity'). As has been emphasised on numerous occasions throughout this book, mental methods should always be seen as a first resort, but if these are not appropriate, then alternatives, such as pencil and paper as well as technology, should be considered. In terms of appropriate use, it is also important for you to understand that technology's significance in mathematics extends beyond its ability to calculate quickly and efficiently. A detailed discussion of this matter lies beyond the scope of this book, but by way of example, it is possible to use calculators with children in Key Stage 1, not as a prop for simple arithmetic, but as a way of exploring number notation, reinforcing the ordering and sequencing of numbers (use the constant function), investigating digit patterns in odd and even numbers and consolidating place value. You might like to explore these possibilities further by consulting some of the sources provided at the end of this chapter.

Learning Outcomes Review

You should now be aware of the messages of research and inspection evidence regarding the utilisation of technology to support arithmetical development over the last thirty years. In particular you should have a clearer understanding of the controversies surrounding the use of calculators and therefore be in a more confident position to make effective use of them in the classroom. You should also have an improved knowledge of the technical aspects of using calculators and spreadsheets, which should allow you to exploit their potential both in your teaching and as part of your wider professional role. All you need to do now is put your new found knowledge and skills to good effect by exploring the constant function or memory facility on your calculator, or by writing a spreadsheet to store and analyse your pupil assessments. Here are some activities that you might like to try first.

Self-assessment questions

1. The square root key on your calculator is broken. Use your calculator to calculate the square root of 28, correct to two decimal places.
2. The multiplication key on your calculator is broken. Use your calculator to calculate 2.875×13.79.
3. Type any number into your calculator. Then carry out the following key presses.

keep cycling through this sequence of five key presses, but have a look at what is in the display after you press the 'equals' key each time. Work through the cycle many times. What do you notice?

Try it again but with a completely different starting number. What do you notice?
Now do the same again, but this time divide by 4 each time. What happens this time?

What happens if you use a divisor of 3 each time?
What happens if you use a divisor of 2?
Can you spot any patterns or connections in your results?

4. Create a spreadsheet that will simulate the calculator activity you have done in question 3. Type your starting number in cell A1 and then type formulae in the cells below which will calculate the answer at the end of each cycle.
   You could have a column that uses division by 2, a column that uses division by 3 and so on.

Further Reading

Andrews, P. (2004) *Mathematical Problem Solving with Interactive Spreadsheets*. Derby: The Association of Teachers of Mathematics.

ATM and MA (no date) *Calculators in the Primary School: Readings from Mathematics in Schools and Mathematics Teaching*. Derby and Leicester: The Association of Teachers of Mathematics and The Mathematical Association.

Bloomfield, A. and Harries, A. (1995) *Teaching, Learning and Mathematics with ICT*. Derby: The Association of Teachers of Mathematics.

English, R. (2006) *Maths and ICT in the Primary School: A Creative Approach*. London: David Fulton Publishers. Chapter 6 ('Using Calculators in Mathematics') provides numerous practical ideas for using calculators in the primary school. There are also many suggestions for spreadsheet activities throughout the rest of the book.

O'Sullivan, L., Harris, A., Sangster, M., Wild, J., Donaldson, G. and Bottle, G. (2005) *Primary Mathematics: Reflective Reader*. London: Learning Matters. Read Chapter 7 ('Making decisions about mathematics and ICT').

Ravenscroft, L., Cobden, D. and Abell, C. (2012) *Mathematical Activities using Spreadsheets*. Leicester: The Mathematical Association.

References

DES (1982) *Mathematics Counts: Report of the Committee of Inquiry into the Teaching of Mathematics in Schools* (The Cockcroft Report). London: HMSO.

DES (1989a) *Mathematics in the National Curriculum*. London: HMSO.

DES (1989b) *Mathematics Non-Statutory Guidance*. London: HMSO.

DfE (2011a) *Use of calculators in primary schools to be reviewed*. DfE press notice, 2 December 2011.

DfE (2011b) *The Framework for the National Curriculum: A report by the Expert Panel for the National Curriculum Review*. London: DfE Publications.

DfE (2012) *National Curriculum for Mathematics: Key Stages 1 and 2 – Draft*. London: DfE Publications.

DfEE (1998) *The Implementation of the National Numeracy Strategy: The Final Report of the Numeracy Task Force*. London: DfEE Publications.

DfEE/QCA (1999) The National Curriculum: Handbook for Primary Teachers in England. London: HMSO.

Girling, M. (1977) Towards a Definition of Basic Numeracy, *Mathematics Teaching*, 81: 4–5.

Ofsted (1993a) *Mathematics Key Stages 1, 2 and 3: Third Year 1991–92*. London: HMSO.

Ofsted (1993b) *The Teaching and Learning of Number in Primary Schools*. London: HMSO.

Ofsted (2000) *The National Numeracy Strategy: The First Year*. London: HMSO.

Ofsted (2002) *The Teaching of Calculation in Primary Schools*. London: HMSO.

Ofsted (2011) *Good Practice in Primary Mathematics: Evidence from 20 successful schools*. Manchester: Ofsted Publications.

Oram, W. J. (1989) *Some notes on CAN and the Suffolk County Mathematics Test*. Ipswich: Suffolk County Council.

Plunkett, S. (1979) 'Decomposition and all that rot', *Mathematics in School*, 8(3): 2–5.

Rowland, T. (1994) *CAN in Suffolk – The Beginnings of a Calculator-Aware Number Curriculum in Three Suffolk Schools* (Homerton Research Report Series). Cambridge: Homerton College Publication Unit.

Ruthven, K. (2001) The English experience of a calculator-aware number curriculum, in Anghileri, J. (ed.) *Principles and Practices in Arithmetic Teaching*. Buckingham: Open University Press.

SCAA (1997) *The Use of Calculators at Key Stages 1–3*. Hayes: SCAA Publications.

Shuard, H., Walsh, A., Goodwin, J. and Worcester, V. (1991) *Calculators, Children and Mathematics*. London: Simon and Schuster.

Appendix: Model answers to the self-assessment questions

Chapter 3

1. If, when calculating 13×25, you partition 13 into 10 and 3 and then multiply each of these by 25, which of the laws of arithmetic are you basing your method on?

You are making use of the distributive law; more specifically, the fact that multiplication by 25 can be distributed over the addition of 10 and 3.

2. If, when calculating $17 \times 5 \times 2$, you work out 5×2 first and then multiply the answer by 17, which of the laws of arithmetic are you basing your method on?

You are making use of the fact that multiplication is associative.

3. Work out the answer to each of the following questions by using an efficient mental method. Make a note of the answer and the method you use.

Possible mental approaches are provided below for each question. The suggestions are listed in order of efficiency, although it is acknowledged that this is very much a matter of personal preference.

　a.　$135 : 5 = 27$

- Divide 135 by 10 and then multiply the answer by 2.
- Multiply 135 by 2 and then divide the answer by 10.
- Partition 135 into 100, 30 and 5, then divide each of these by 5, and finally add the three answers (20, 6 and 1) together.

b.　$38 + 26 + 26 = 90$

- Double 26 to give 52 and then add this to 38.
- Partition the three numbers, then work out $30 + 20 + 20 = 70$ and $8 + 6 + 6 = 20$, and finally add the two answers together.
- Work from left to right, adding 38 and 26 (this can be done in various ways, for example using partitioning, or near multiples of 10) and then adding 26 to the answer.

c.　$5004 - 1947 = 3057$

- Count on from 1947 to 5004, for example from 1947 to 2000 (53), then 2000 to 5000 (3000), then 5000 to 5004 (4).
- Count back from 5004 to 1947, in a similar fashion to the above but backwards.

d. $33 \times 7 \times 3 = 693$

- Multiply 33 by 3 to give 99. Then multiply this by 7 by actually working out 100×7 and subtracting 7 from the answer.
- Multiply 7 by 3 to give 21. Then multiply this by 33 by working out 10×33, doubling the answer and finally adding 33.
- Multiply 33 by 7 (possibly by partitioning) and then multiply the answer by 3 (again, possibly by partitioning).

Chapter 4

Answer the following questions using any approaches you wish, apart from the traditional compact pencil and paper methods.

1. $714 - 368$

You could use the ENL to count on from the lower number to the higher number, as shown below.

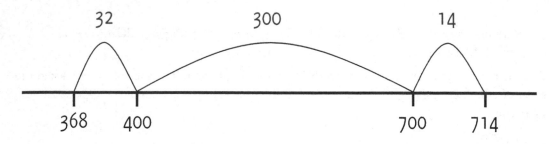

Alternatively, you could count on, recording the steps, but without drawing the number line.

$714 - 368 =$
  368
    (+32)
  400
    (+300)
  700
    (+14)
  714
  (Total 346)

2. $837 + 588$

You could use an expanded horizontal method based on partitioning.

$$837 + 588 = 1300 + 110 + 15$$
$$= 1425$$

Alternatively, you could use an expanded vertical layout.

```
   837
+  588
  1300
   110
+   15
  1425
```

Another possibility is to recognise that 588 is a near multiple of 100 and so add 600 and then subtract 12 to compensate, as shown below.

$$
\begin{aligned}
837 + 588 &= 837 + 600 - 12 \\
&= 1437 - 12 \\
&= 1425
\end{aligned}
$$

3. 43×517

You could use the grid method, as shown below.

×	40	3
500	20,000	1500
10	400	30
7	280	21

The six answers then have to be added together, possibly by adding the rows, or alternatively the columns, or by looking for numbers that can be combined efficiently. Whichever approach is used, it is likely that intermediate answers will have to be jotted down. (Answer = 22,231)

4. $1049 \div 37$ (use remainders rather than decimals)

You could use the chunking method, based on a combination of multiplication and subtraction, as shown below.

```
        28
37 )1049
  -  370        (10 × 37)
     679
     370        (10 × 37)
     309
  -  185        (5 × 37)
     124
  -  111        (3 × 37)
      13
```

$1049 \div 37 = 28$ remainder 13

Chapter 5

Answer the following questions using the traditional compact pencil and paper methods that have been discussed in this chapter.

1. $714 - 368$

Just in case you need it, here is a step-by-step breakdown of how you should have tackled it using the traditional method.

Step 1

$$\begin{array}{r} 7\ ^0\cancel{1}\ ^14 \\ -\ 3\ 6\ 8 \\ \hline 6 \end{array}$$

You cannot subtract 8 from 4, so borrow 10 from the adjacent column to leave 0 tens (cross out the 1 and replace with 0). The 4 ones now becomes 14. Subtract 8 from 14 to leave 6.

Step 2

$$\begin{array}{r} ^6\cancel{7}\ ^{10}\cancel{1}\ ^14 \\ -3\ 6\ 8 \\ \hline 4\ 6 \end{array}$$

You cannot subtract 6 from 0 in the tens column, so borrow 100 from the 7 hundreds in the adjacent column, to leave 6 hundreds (cross out the 7 and replace with 6). The 0 tens now becomes 10 tens.
Subtract 6 from 10 to leave 4.

Step 3

$$\begin{array}{r} ^6\cancel{7}\ ^{10}\cancel{1}\ ^14 \\ -3\ 6\ 8 \\ \hline 3\ 4\ 6 \end{array}$$

Finally, in the hundreds column, subtract 3 from 6 to leave 3.

2. $837 + 588$

Here is a step-by-step breakdown of the traditional 'carrying' method.

Step 1

$$\begin{array}{r} 8\ 3\ 7 \\ +\ 5\ 8_1\ 8 \\ \hline 5 \end{array}$$

7 add 8 equals 15.
'Carry' the 1 in the tens column and write down the 5 ones.

Step 2

$$\begin{array}{r} 8\ 3\ 7 \\ +\ 5_1\ 8_1\ 8 \\ \hline 2\ 5 \end{array}$$

3 add 8 add 1 equals 12.
'Carry' the 1 in the hundreds column and write down the 2 tens.

Step 3

$$\begin{array}{r} 8\ 3\ 7 \\ +\ 5_1\ 8_1\ 8 \\ \hline 1\ 4\ 2\ 5 \end{array}$$

8 add 5 add 1 equals 14.
Write down the 14 hundreds.

3. 43×517

Here is a step-by-step breakdown of the traditional method for long multiplication.

Step 1

```
      5 1 7
×       4₂ 3
    1 5 5 1
```

Multiply 517 by 3, using short multiplication to give the answer 1551.

Step 2

```
      5 1 7
×     2 4₂ 3
    1 5 5 1
  2 0 6 8 0
```

Multiply 517 by 40, by first writing down a zero and then multiplying by 4 using short multiplication.
The answer, 20680, is written below 1551.

Step 3

```
      5 1 7
×     2 4₂ 3
    1 5 5 1
  2 0₁6 ₁8 0
  2 2 2 3 1
```

Add 1551 and 20680 using the traditional method for addition.

4. $1049 \div 37$ (use remainders rather than decimals)

Here is a step-by-step breakdown of the traditional method for long division.

Step 1

```
          2
37 )1 0 4 9
```

104 divided by 37 is 2.
Write down the 2 above the line. Calculate the remainder in step 2.

Step 2

```
          2
37 )1 0 4 9
   − 7 4
      3 0
```

2 multiplied by 37 is 74. Write down 74 below 104.
Subtract 74 from 104 to give the remainder 30.

Step 3

```
         2 8
37 )1 0 4 9
   − 7 4 ↓
      3 0 9
```

Drop the 9 down so that it appears after the 30.
309 divided by 37 equals 8.
Write down the 8 above the line.
Calculate the remainder in step 4.

Step 4

$$
\begin{array}{r}
2\,8 \\
37\,\overline{)1\,0\,4\,9} \\
-\,7\,4\downarrow \\
\hline
3\,0\,9 \\
-\,2\,9\,6 \\
\hline
1\,3
\end{array}
$$

8 multiplied by 37 is 296. Write down 296 below 309.
Subtract 296 from 309 to give the remainder 13.

The answer is 28 remainder 13.

Chapter 6

1. Tom and Sally each start with the same amount of money. Tom spends two-thirds of his. Sally spends five-sixths of hers. In total they have £12 left. How much did they each have at the start?

Tom spends two-thirds, so he must have one-third left.

Sally spends five-sixths, so she must have one-sixth left.

One third (which is equivalent to two-sixths), plus one-sixth equals three-sixths, which is one-half.

So one-half is £12 and therefore the original amount was £24.

They each had £24 at the start.

2. Use an efficient method to calculate the following.

   a. 9.8 − 7.75 = 2.05

An efficient mental method would be to think of it in terms of money and so it becomes £9.80 − £7.75. Then subtract 75p from 80p, and £7 from £9.

Another possibility would be to count up from 7.75 to 9.8 using an ENL, or simply jotting down the steps.

   b. 20 × 3.875 = 77.5

An efficient mental method would be to multiply 3.875 by 10 and then double the answer. Alternatively, double 3.875 and then multiply the answer by 10.

3. A coat is reduced by 20% in the sale. The sale price is £60. What was the original price?

A common error would be to add back 20% of £60. The important thing to be aware of is that the reduction was 20% of the original price, not 20% of £60.

If the original price was reduced by 20%, then the sale price, £60, represents the remainder, i.e. 80% of the original price.

So if 80% of the original price is £60
then 20% of the original price is £15
therefore the original price must have been £75.
You can check this by reducing £75 by 20%, to see if this gives the correct sale price.

4. A model aircraft is made using the scale 1:72.

  a. The propeller of the model has a diameter of 2.5cm. What is the diameter of the real
  propeller?

Model aircraft	:	Actual aircraft
1	:	72
2.5cm	:	2.5cm x 72
2.5cm	:	180cm

The real aircraft's propeller is 180cm or 1.8m in diameter.

  b. The wingspan of the real aircraft is 20 metres. What is the wingspan of the model? (You
  can use a calculator for this part of the question.)

Model aircraft	:	Actual aircraft
1	:	72 (Divide both numbers by 72 to create an equivalent ratio.)
0.0139	:	1
$0.0139 \times 20m$	:	20m
0.278m	:	20m

The model aircraft's wingspan is 0.278m or 27.8cm (correct to 3 significant figures).

Chapter 7

1. The square root key on your calculator is broken. Use your calculator to calculate the square
root of 28, correct to two decimal places.

You probably used trial and improvement skills in conjunction with estimation to solve this
one. $5^2 = 25$ and $6^2 = 36$, so possibly try 5.5 as a first estimate, although you may have chosen
a number closer to 5 than 6 because 28 is closer to 25 than 36.

5.5^2	=	30.25	Too big
5.3^2	=	28.09	Too big
5.2^2	=	27.04	Too small
5.25^2	=	27.5625	Too small
5.28^2	=	27.8784	Too small
5.29^2	=	27.9841	Too small
5.295^2	=	28.037025	Too big
5.292^2	=	28.005264	Too big

You do not need to go any further with this because the final answer only has to be correct to two decimal places. The choice is therefore between 5.29 and 5.30 and from the final calculation above it is clear that the answer must be closer to 5.29.

2. The multiplication key on your calculator is broken. Use your calculator to calculate 2.875×13.79.

One possibility is to use the inverse relationship between multiplication and division.

If $\quad 2.875 \times 13.79 = X$

Then $\qquad 2.875 = X \div 13.79$

You could use trial and improvement methods to eventually find the answer.

Another possibility is to use your knowledge of fractions and decimals equivalents and the fact that 2.875 is $2\frac{7}{8}$. You can also make use of the distributive law and the memory facility, as discussed in Chapter 7.

$2.875 \times 13.79 = (2 \times 13.79) + (0.875 \times 13.79)$

Use the M+ key to add two lots of 13.79 to the memory.

Then divide 13.79 by 8 to give $\frac{1}{8}$.

Use the M+ key to add seven lots of this to the memory i.e. $\frac{7}{8}$.

Press the MR key to display the answer.

A slight variation is to think of 2.875 lots as 3 lots minus 0.125 lots.

$2.875 \times 13.79 = (3 \times 13.79) - (0.125 \times 13.79)$

Use the M+ key to add three lots of 13.79 to the memory.

Then divide 13.79 by 8 to give $\frac{1}{8}$.

Use the M− key to subtract one lot of this from the memory i.e. $\frac{1}{8}$.

Press the MR key to display the answer.

3. Type any number into your calculator. Then carry out the following key presses.

| ÷ | 5 | + | 1 | = | ÷ | 5 | + | 1 | = |

Keep cycling through this sequence of five key presses, but have a look at what is in the display after you press the 'equals' key each time. Work through the cycle many times. What do you notice?

Try it again but with a completely different starting number. What do you notice?

Now do the same again, but this time divide by 4 each time. What happens this time?

What happens if you use a divisor of 3 each time?

What happens if you use a divisor of 2?

Can you spot any patterns or connections in your results?

When dividing by 5 the answers converge on 1.25, regardless of the starting number.

When dividing by 4 the answers converge on 1.333.

When dividing by 3 the answers converge on 1.5.

When dividing by 2 the answers converge on 2.

The patterns and relationships in these results are illustrated in the table below.

Divisor	Converges on (decimal)	Converges on (fraction)
2	2.0	2
3	1.5	1½
4	1.333	1⅓
5	1.25	1¼
6	1.2	1⅕

By writing the answers as fractions it might become easier to spot the pattern. You can probably predict that when dividing by 7 the answers will converge on 1⅙ or 1.167 as a decimal.

4. Create a spreadsheet that will simulate the calculator activity you have done in question 3. Type your starting number in cell A1 and then type formulae in the cells below which will calculate the answer at the end of each cycle.

You could have a column that uses division by 2, a column that uses division by 3 and so on.

For division by 2, type any number (for example 25) into cell A1 and then into cell A2 type the formula

=A1/2+1

Then copy this formula down the column as far as you want, say as far as row 20.

For division by 3, type any number into cell B1 and then type into cell B2 the formula

=B1/3+1

Similarly in columns C, D, E and F use the formulae

=C1/4+1

=D1/5+1

=E1/6+1

=F1/7+1

The results displayed in the cells will look something like this.

	A	B	C	D	E	F
1	25	62	108	49	54	97
2	13.5	21.667	28	10.8	10	14.857
3	7.75	8.2222	8	3.16	2.6667	3.1224
4	4.875	3.7407	3	1.632	1.4444	1.4461
5	3.4375	2.2469	1.75	1.3264	1.2407	1.2066
6	2.7188	1.7490	1.4375	1.2653	1.2068	1.1724
7	2.3594	1.5829	1.3594	1.2531	1.2011	1.1675
8	2.1797	1.5277	1.3398	1.2506	1.2002	1.1668
9	2.0898	1.5092	1.3349	1.2501	1.2	1.1667
10	2.0449	1.5031	1.3337	1.25	1.2	1.1667
11	2.0225	1.5010	1.3334	1.25	1.2	1.1667
12	2.0112	1.5003	1.3334	1.25	1.2	1.1667
13	2.0056	1.5001	1.3333	1.25	1.2	1.1667
14	2.0028	1.5	1.3333	1.25	1.2	1.1667

Index

addition
  chunking using 60–1
  fractions problems involving 96–7
  informal pencil and paper strategies 46–9
  laws of arithmetic 33
  mental calculation strategies 26–9
  traditional pencil and paper methods 68–70
  see also complementary addition; equal
    addition; repeated addition
addition doubles 55
algorithms, traditional 6, 67–8, 108
Anghileri, J. 61
approximation 123–4
arithmetic
  attainment in 11
  children's decision-making in 43–4
  current issues and challenges 11–12
  curriculum *see* curriculum
  definitions 3–4
  flexible approach to 6, 10
  government priorities 9–10
  laws of 33–6
  operations
    awareness of relationships between 12, 26
    see also addition; division; multiplication;
      subtraction
  progression in 41–2, 43, 66, 87
  skills 11, 12, 37, 38
  teaching *see* teaching
  use of term 5
  using technology *see* technology
arithmetical fluency 43
arrays 43
Askew, W. 17
associative law 32, 34–5
attainment *see* children's attainment; progression

base 10 blocks 65, 77–8
Beishuizen, M. 47
Board of Education Report (1925) 3–4
'borrowing' method (subtraction) 70–4
'borrowing and paying back' method (subtraction)
  74–6
Boulton-Lewis, G.M. 77
Bramald, R. 32
built-in functions (spreadsheet) 129

Calculator-Aware Number (CAN) 117, 119–22
calculators
  C, AC and CE keys 124
  constant function 124
  displaying large numbers 125–6
  historical background 116–18
  interpreting displays 128
  memory facility 126–7
  precedence of operations 125
  role, in relation to progression 87
  using
    confusion regarding 119
    with fractions, decimals and percentages 92
'cancelling down' (fractions) 91
'carrying' method (addition) 68–70
children's attainment, in arithmetic 11, 120
children's errors
  addition 69–70
  division 84
  multiplication 79, 80–1
  subtraction 72–4
  using to introduce efficient mental strategies 25
chunking 43, 59–61, 105
co-operative learning 25, 38
Cockcroft Report (1982) 3, 11, 117
column value (in place value) 32–3
common denominators 91, 97, 99
'common sense' approach 101, 110, 113
commutative law 32, 33
complementary addition 50, 54, 103
confidence, in mental arithmetic 25
constant function (calculator) 124
counting
  importance in mental arithmetic 38
  over-dependence on 17
counting back 49–50
counting up 50–1
cross-curricular mathematics 24
curriculum 4
  statutory requirements 7–9, 18, 19, 89–90
  see also National Curriculum

data (spreadsheet) 129
decimals
  arithmetic with 101–6
  equivalent forms 92

importance of models and images 93
what children need to know 92
decision-making, in arithmetic by children 43–4
decomposition, subtraction by 70–4, 104
deduction skills 17
denominators 91, 108
see also common denominators
Department for Education 41–2, 66
'derive', in recall of number facts 17–18
Dienes' base 10 blocks 77–8
difference, subtraction as 49–51
discussion-based lessons 25–6, 38
distributive law 32, 33–4
dividend 35, 36, 59
division
fractions problems involving 97–100
informal pencil and paper strategies 59–61
laws of arithmetic 33, 34, 35
mental calculation strategies 29–32
research into written methods for 61
tradition pencil and paper methods 83–5
divisors 35, 36, 59, 83
doubling 31, 55–6
'drill and practice' software 20

efficient mental arithmetic
addition and subtraction 28–9
multiplication and division 31–2
efficient written methods 42, 43
Egyptian multiplication 56, 82–3
empty number line, using
for addition 46–7
with decimals 103
for subtraction 49
equal addition, subtraction by 74–6
equal parts (fractions) 91
equivalence, subtraction using 51
equivalent calculation combinations 32
equivalent fractions 91, 93
equivalent ratios 112
errors *see* children's errors
estimation 123–4
'exchanging' (subtraction), use of term 71
expanded horizontal approaches, using
for addition 48
with decimals 102, 104
for multiplication 56
expanded vertical approaches, using
for addition 48–9
with decimals 102, 104
for multiplication 56–7

false generalisations 95
'feel for number' 16–17, 36, 37
Final Report of the Numeracy Task Force 4
'for every' expression (ratios) 93
formal written methods
use of term 10
see also traditional pencil and paper arithmetic
formulae (spreadsheet) 129
fractional parts 100
fractions
children's misconceptions (case study) 94–5
children's difficulties with 91
creating from a presented scenario 95–6
equivalent forms 92
importance of models and images 93
problems and computation 101
problems involving arithmetic operations 96–100
what children need to know 91
Framework for Teaching Mathematics (1999) 5, 41

games 20
GCSE mathematics 11
Gibb, N. 5, 121
Girling, M. 116–17
Gove, M. 5
Gray, E. 17
'grid' method (multiplication) 57–8, 105

Hart, K. 77, 101
Houssart, J. 77
100 squares 43

ICT 20
see also technology
images, importance of 93
informal pencil and paper arithmetic 9, 41–62
addition 46–9
decimals 102, 103, 104, 105–6
division 59–61
engaging parents in developing 44
first stages of (case study) 44–5
freedom of decision-making in 43–4
government position on 10, 42, 43
multiplication 55–8
progression in 41–2, 43
resources 43
subtraction 49–54
using and applying 44
instrumental understanding 6, 7, 86

see also procedural fluency
integers 112, 113
Interactive Teaching Programs 20
interactive whiteboards, using 93
investigation/investigative tasks 12, 38, 119, 120, 133, 134

Jarvin, L. 77
jottings 43, 44–5

Key Stage 2, test results 11
Kieren, T.E. 91
known facts
    distinguishing between mental arithmetic and 16–17
    expanding through practice 26

laws of arithmetic 33–6
'left to right' approach (addition) 48
long division 83, 84–5, 106
long multiplication 78, 79–83

McIntosh, A. 4
McNeil, N.M. 77
Mathematical Association report (1954) 4
mathematical concepts, need for understanding of 42
mathematical understanding 4, 6–7, 12
measure(s)
    decimal link with 92
    in fractions 91
memory facility (calculator) 126–7
mental agility 24
mental arithmetic 24–40
    curricular requirements 8
    with decimals 102, 103, 104, 105
    distinguishing between known facts and 16–17
    equipping children for 36–8
    as the first resort 38–9, 43
    fractions problems 97
    implications for teaching *see* teaching
    importance of discussion 25–6
    lack of government reference to 10
    laws of arithmetic 33–6
    model of 37–8
    status of mental methods 24–5
    strategies
        for addition and subtraction 26–9
        for multiplication and division 29–32
        place value 32–3
mental methods 24–5

mental modelling 43
mental skills, using and applying 38
model(s)
    importance of 93
    of mental calculation 37–8
Mooney, C. 91
multiplication
    chunking using 59–61
    fractions problems involving 97
    informal pencil and paper strategies 55–8
    jottings to support (case study) 44–5
    laws of arithmetic 33–4
    mental calculation strategies 29–32
    tables (case study) 21–2
    traditional pencil and paper methods 78–83
multipliers 78, 91

National Curriculum (1989) 7, 8, 17, 117, 118
National Curriculum (2000) 8, 9
National Curriculum (2011) 9, 10
National Numeracy Project 4
National Numeracy Strategy 4, 8, 41, 77, 89, 118, 119
National Strategies 5, 20, 41, 89
negative numbers, vertical subtraction using 52
Netherlands
    use of the empty number line 47
    written methods for division 61
'no hands' approaches 26
non-calculator methods 8, 9
Nuffield Mathematics Teaching Project 4
number facts, recall *see* rapid recall of number facts
number lines 43, 93
number sense 16–17, 36, 37
number system 36–7
numeracy 4–5, 116–17
Numeracy Framework 4
Numeracy Task Force 118
numerators 91, 108

Ofsted, comments about calculators 119
operator, component of fractions 91
oral-mental starters 24
Oram, W.J. 120
O'Sullivan, L. 68
ownership, of mathematics 44, 51, 65

parents, engaging 19, 44
'part-whole' component of fractions 91
partitioning 32

see also expanded horizontal approaches;
   expanded vertical approaches
partitioning cards 43
'parts per hundred' (percentages) 92, 109
pedagogical issues, using technology 134
pedagogical knowledge 12
pencil and paper arithmetic
   curricular requirements 8–9
   see also informal pencil and paper arithmetic;
      traditional pencil and paper arithmetic
percentage parts 107–11
percentages 92
   creating from a presented scenario 107
   equivalent forms 92
   importance of models and images 93
place value 32–3, 43, 77, 92
place value cards 93
Plowden Report (1967) 4
Plunkett, S. 67–8, 87, 117
presentation issues, spreadsheets 130
presented scenarios
   creating fractions from 95–6
   creating percentages from 107
Primary Framework for Mathematics 17
Primary National Strategy 119
Primary Strategies 8
problem solving 12, 38, 43, 101, 119, 120, 122,
   123, 133, 134
procedural fluency 42, 86
   see also instrumental understanding
programmes of study 8, 9, 10, 18, 42, 66, 90
progression, in arithmetic 41–2, 43, 66, 87
proportion, ratio and 93
pupil-centred education 4

quantity value (in place value) 32–3
questioning, recall of number facts 20
quotient, component of fractions 91

rapid recall of number facts 15–23
   broad principles 18–19
   curricular requirements 7, 18, 19
   implications for teaching *see* teaching
   and mental arithmetic
      distinguishing between known facts 16–17
      as a prerequisite for 36
   trainee teachers' development in 22
   what children need to know 17–18
ratio(s) 93
   arithmetic with 110–13
   component in fractions 91

importance of models and images 93
   and proportion 93
Realistic Mathematics Education (RME) initiative
   47
reasoning 43, 133
reciprocal 98
relational awareness, between arithmetic operations
   12, 26
relational understanding 6, 7, 77, 86
remainders, in division 83, 84, 85
repeated addition 55, 59, 97
repeated doubling 31, 55–6
repeated halving 31
repeated subtraction 59, 61, 99
resources 12, 20, 25, 43, 77–8, 93
'right to left' approach (addition) 48
Rowland, T. 120
Ruthven, K. 120

'same difference' method (subtraction) 51
'scaling down' 91, 93, 112
'scaling up' 91, 93, 107, 108, 112
'separate tens' (1010) approach 47
'sequence tens' (N10) approach 47
short division 83–4, 85
short multiplication 78–9, 105
Skemp, R. 6, 7
songs, use of 20
spreadsheets
   built-in functions 129
   defined 128–9
   formulae 129
   presentation issues 130
   ways of using 131–3
subject knowledge 12, 26, 42, 44, 82, 86, 95,
   113–14
subtraction
   chunking using 59–60
   fractions problems involving 99
   informal pencil and paper strategies 49–54
   laws of arithmetic 33, 34
   mental calculation strategies 26–9
   traditional pencil and paper methods 70–6
   see also repeated subtraction

'taking away', subtraction as 49, 54
talk partners 25
teaching
   criticism of 11
   fractions, decimals, percentages and ratios 113
   mental arithmetic

importance of counting 38
    using and applying mental skills 38
rapid recall of number facts
    case study 21–2
    extending children's learning 20
    providing opportunities for 19
    questioning 20
    resources 20
traditional pencil and paper arithmetic
    guiding principles 66–7
    implications for 86
using technology
    appropriate use 134
    effective use of calculators 12
    pedagogical issues 134
    technological issues 133–4
technology, arithmetic using 116–35
    appropriate use 122, 134
    historical background 116–21
    implications for teaching see teaching
    knowledge required for
        appropriate use of 122
        importance of estimation and
            approximation 123–4
        interpreting results 123
        technical aspects 122
        understanding what needs to be calculated
            122–3
    spreadsheets 128–33
    teaching see teaching
    what children need to know 121–4
    see also calculators; ICT
'think-pair-share' 25

thinking time 25, 26
Thompson, I. 32, 37–8, 47
traditional algorithms 6, 67–8, 108
traditional pencil and paper arithmetic 64–88
    addition 68–70
    benefits 64–5
    decimals 103, 104, 105, 106
    division
        long 83, 84–5, 106
        short 83–4, 85
    fractions problems 96–7, 97–8
    ineffectiveness of early introduction 41
    multiplication
        long 78, 79–83
        short 78–9, 105
    percentages 108
    potential difficulties 65–6
    research, use of base 10 blocks 77–8
    subtraction
        by decomposition 70–4
        by equal addition 74–6
    teaching see teaching

vertical subtraction, using negative numbers 52
visual resources/images 12, 77, 93

Wiliam, D. 17
Williams Review (2008) 24, 25
word problems 122
written methods
    terminology 9, 10
    see also pencil and paper arithmetic